Early Praise for *Serverless Apps on Cloudflare*

As someone interested in all things serverless, and constantly curious about new technologies, Cloudflare was top of my list of technologies to explore. Ashley's book does an incredible job of walking through, step by step, how to get started building serverless apps on Cloudflare. And Ashley does all of that using practical examples that I can take directly and use in real-world applications saving me countless hours. A must-have for anyone interested in Cloudflare, or anyone building modern serverless applications in general.

➤ James Eastham
   Serverless DA, Datadog

Cloud computing has never been more relevant, and serverless is the natural next evolution of this technology. This book provides everything you need to get started with serverless and Cloudflare, explained in a concise, entertaining way, with excellent examples to really guide the start of your serverless journey.

➤ Adam Cox
   Software Test Engineer, Simply Business

This book is a great introduction to Cloudflare and serverless with detailed step-by-step examples, and everything is well explained. Well worth a read for anyone looking to learn more about this exciting new technology.

➤ Kelvin Samuel
   Software Engineer, Simply Business

This book has been a fantastic introduction to severless as a concept and Cloudflare as a tool. I knew little about either, and since completing the book I've been able to build serverless applications both on side projects and in my day job.

➤ Robert Faldo
   Senior Software Engineer, Simply Business

Serverless Apps on Cloudflare

Build Solutions, Not Infrastructure

Ashley Peacock

The Pragmatic Bookshelf

Dallas, Texas

For our complete catalog of hands-on, practical, and Pragmatic content for software developers, please visit *https://pragprog.com*.

Contact *support@pragprog.com* for sales, volume licensing, and support.

For international rights, please contact *rights@pragprog.com*.

The team that produced this book includes:

Publisher:	Dave Thomas
COO:	Janet Furlow
Executive Editor:	Susannah Davidson
Development Editor:	Michael Swaine
Copy Editor:	Vanya Wryter
Indexing:	Potomac Indexing, LLC

ISBN-13: 979-8-88865-071-4
Book version: P1.0—November 2024

Contents

Acknowledgments

In the first book that I wrote, I started the acknowledgments by saying I never thought I'd write a book. The same is true when it comes to the second book: I never thought I'd write a second book either. On top of that, this book is significantly longer than the first; it blows my mind even now that I was able to write well over 50,000 words about Cloudflare.

I couldn't have done it alone though. I'd like to thank The Pragmatic Bookshelf for once again believing in my vision for the book, and believing in me as an author. Special thanks to Michael Swaine, who once again edited my book, and had to deal with my many questions and emails throughout the eighteen months it took to write the book.

I'd also like to thank those who reviewed my book: Adam Cox, Kelvin Samuel, and Rob Faldo. Their feedback and bug finding were essential in making the book as polished, complete, and digestible as possible.

It goes without saying that there'd be no book without Cloudflare. I want to thank everyone at Cloudflare who brought their developer platform to life, to challenge the status quo set by the likes of AWS, Azure, and GCP. I wrote this book because I believe their platform is incredibly powerful and primarily built with engineers in mind, empowering them to build the best applications they can in the shortest amount of time possible. Not only that, it continues to grow at an astonishing rate. I can't wait to see how it develops in the future.

Penultimately, I want to thank and acknowledge my wife, Lia. She is steadfast in her support, and has always been inquisitive throughout the process. From giving me the time and space to write the book, to always asking how it's going and what's left to do, her interest and support has meant the world. Lia, I thank you from the bottom of my heart.

To round out, I want to thank my family for all they have ever done for me. Without their care, love, and support, I wouldn't be the person I am today. I wouldn't have made it as far as I have in life. I'll be forever grateful for everything they've ever done for me, and continue to do for me. I'm truly thankful.

Preface

Welcome reader, and future Cloudflare and serverless master!

This book is all about Cloudflare's developer platform and serverless. I've used the platform extensively, and advocated for others to explore its offering. I believe its platform is the best out there for building applications on, with some of, if not the best, developer experience of any major cloud platform.

Who Should Read This Book?

This book is primarily aimed at anyone working with software and application development. Whether you're an engineer, architect, or CTO, you'll find plenty to sink your teeth into in this book.

If you've been using the likes of AWS and Azure, I think you'll find Cloudflare a breath of fresh air. If you want to try something completely different, that streamlines your development process, and in a way that enables you as a developer, this is the book for you.

Similarly, if you're new to serverless, you'll find this book serves as an excellent introduction. The simplicity of Cloudflare's platform allows you to focus on learning the fundamentals, without worrying about the complexities that come with building on other cloud platforms.

What's in This Book?

We'll start with an overview of what serverless is, before diving straight into deploying your first application to Cloudflare's platform. Through the course of the book, we'll cover all the essential building blocks that are needed to build modern web applications. To give you a flavor of what will be covered, here are some highlights:

- Deploying Workers, Cloudflare's serverless compute.
- Building static and full-stack applications; connecting to databases, object storage, caches, and more.

- Implementing AI using Workers AI, Cloudflare's globally-distributed inference platform.
- Building asynchronous applications with serverless message queues.
- Deploying real-time applications that use WebSockets in just a few lines of code.

By the end, you'll be able to build almost any kind of application using Cloudflare.

How to Read This Book

The book is structured into five distinct sections. Each chapter focuses on a specific aspect of the Cloudflare platform, going into detail about the primary features of each product.

You'll start out by building an API using Workers, moving on to building static and full stack applications next, then building another full stack application, this time using object storage and AI, but building it in an event-driven way. Lastly, you'll build a real-time chat application using WebSockets, with the book finishing up by covering automated deployments and preparing your application for production.

Online Resources

The source code used in this book is available online at the Pragmatic Book-shelf website.[1] You'll find a link to the book forum there, which is your place to talk with other readers and with us. If you find any mistakes, please report them on the errata page. And I can be reached here:

- Email: ashley@technicalbookclub.com
- Twitter: @_ashleypeacock

Now, let's get building with Cloudflare and serverless!

---

1. https://pragprog.com/titles/apapps/serverless-apps-on-cloudflare/

Introduction

Back when I started creating software, over fifteen years ago, things looked very different to how they do now. I started out like a lot of engineers, building a simple blog using PHP and MySQL. It was the perfect introduction to programming, with the ability to simply upload your PHP code to some cheap, shared hosting, and instantly be able to run your code.

There were no containers, and nobody had really heard of the cloud, with Amazon just starting its journey with AWS. As the cloud took off, and everyone started migrating, technologies such as Docker became increasingly popular, allowing you to run your applications locally inside containers, and deploy those same containers remotely in the cloud.

At each point, the idea has been to make building and deploying applications simpler and easier for everyone. Right now, you can go and spin up quite literally anything in the cloud, from your own instances, to databases, to machine learning tools, and everything in between.

The next big shift in how we build and deploy applications, in my opinion, is serverless.

What is Serverless?

With serverless, you don't pay for what you don't use. That's a big deal. I'll explain.

The most common way to deploy applications to the cloud today is to provision an instance, such as on AWS EC2, and then deploy your application to it. Whether you put the code on there directly, or via containers using AWS ECS, you're ultimately renting servers from the cloud provider, and paying for every hour your instance is running. Considering your websites can be accessed 24/7, that means your EC2 instances are also running 24/7, and you're paying 24/7.

With serverless, you package up your code, upload it to a serverless runtime, and the cloud provider handles the rest. You don't need to provision any servers, your code is simply executed when a request comes in. If your website receives zero requests in twenty-four hours, you'd pay $0 because your application didn't handle any requests.

Imagine your application hasn't received any requests for a while. Then, a single HTTP request comes in. Your application's code will be loaded into memory, the request will be executed against it, and a response returned. Imagine a second request comes in right after; it'll potentially be executed against that same instance of your serverless function, or perhaps a new instance will be created. After a period of that application receiving no requests, the code will be removed from memory, and another instance will be created when the next request comes in.

For some cloud providers, when a request comes in and a new instance of your serverless application is needed, this can sometimes be a little slow, as it has to load your application into memory. It varies depending on the language and runtime, but these initial loads can often take upwards of 500 milliseconds.

With Cloudflare, cold starts are not generally an issue, thanks to their platform being geared entirely towards serverless. When a request is made from a client, such as a browser, it must first establish a secure connection (as pretty much everything these days is over a secure connection, such as HTTPS). This process is known as the TLS handshake, and during that handshake, the client must send a "hello" message to whoever it's trying to connect to. When Cloudflare sees that hello, it knows what code to load to serve that request based on the URL. It loads that code in memory ready to go during the TLS handshake, so when the handshake completes and it needs to handle the actual request, there's no wait time for your code to load.

I'm going to focus on the Cloudflare serverless platform in this book, but the serverless concept is agnostic of any cloud provider. Every cloud provider has a serverless offering, so you can apply what you learn in this book to any of those platforms. Although the implementation details will differ, the underlying serverless approach you'll learn here will work anywhere.

I'm a serverless fan, and as I see it, serverless benefits you in four ways: pay for what you use, scalability, high availability, and no server maintenance. I'll discuss each of these with Cloudflare as my example, but the benefits apply to any serverless solution.

Pay for What You Use

With the major cloud providers, you effectively pay per request handled. Each request handled by your serverless function is called an invocation. That might sound expensive, and it can be if you get a lot of requests, but for the vast majority of websites and applications, your costs won't get anywhere near what they would if you were provisioning your own instances.

Take Cloudflare, for example; you can sign up for a free account, and instantly get access to 100,000 free requests per day. If your website becomes popular enough to hit that limit, you'll only pay $0.50 per million invocations after that. Considering the cheapest EC2 instance from AWS, at the time of writing, is around $50 a month, you'd need your EC2 instance to serve a lot of requests before it would be more cost-effective to run on EC2. In fact, you'd need to handle over a hundred million requests through Cloudflare before you reach the same spend as a single EC2 instance on AWS.

However, if you were receiving enough requests to make an EC2 instance more cost-effective than serverless, I doubt the smallest EC2 instance would handle that. In the example above, assuming the hundred million requests were spread out evenly, your single EC2 instance would have to handle thirty-eight requests per second, which is a tall ask for a single EC2 instance with limited resources.

That brings us nicely to the next principle of serverless: built-in scalability.

Scalability

As your application grows and becomes more popular, you'll receive more traffic to it. That will raise the amount of CPU and memory your application uses, and at some point, you won't have enough to handle all the requests. You can extract a lot from a single EC2 instance, especially if you use concurrency, but it will only go so far.

In a traditional cloud setup, you have two options in order to handle more traffic: vertical or horizontal scaling. Vertical scaling involves increasing the resources on your instances, whereas horizontal scaling increases the number of instances you have running.

In both cases, there's naturally a cost increase. Increasing the instance type on your EC2 instance, even from the smallest to the second smallest, doubles your monthly cost. Each time you increase the size of your instance in AWS, the cost roughly doubles. If you need more memory, you have no real choice but to increase the instance type (unless you can optimize your application's memory use). Along the same lines, adding more instances and horizontally scaling increases costs too. And don't forget about the additional cost of load balancers.

If we compare that to serverless, a lot of that complexity is handled for you. You might still need to pick how much memory you want to allocate, or how much CPU, but that's about it. With Cloudflare, there are set limits for CPU and memory. Each instance of your serverless function has 128MB of memory to work with, and as much CPU as you could realistically need.

Even on the free plan, you get 10ms of CPU time per request. It might not sound like a lot, but in terms of CPU time, the vast majority of requests to Cloudflare use less than 1ms of CPU time. That doesn't mean your application has to respond in 10ms, as a lot of what an application might do isn't CPU-related. For example, waiting for a response from an API call or writing data to a database. I've yet to hit any of these limits when developing applications on Cloudflare.

As we're now just packaging up code and giving it to the cloud to handle, we don't worry about servers, and your serverless applications will automatically scale to meet demand, without any work from you. Additionally, in the case of Cloudflare, you don't need to worry about load balancers either, or even how to expose your application; it's all handled for you, including DNS and SSL certificates.

That means if your application gets a surge of traffic, which can sometimes unexpectedly happen, your application will scale to meet demand. There's no configuration needed; unlike when you horizontally scale your own instances, serverless has auto-scaling built-in.

In the traditional cloud setup, there's actually a second reason to run multiple containers besides scalability, and that brings us on to the third principle of serverless: high availability.

High Availability

High availability and scalability are closely linked, as they are both key to ensuring your application is always ready to meet the needs of your users. Whereas scalability is all about ensuring your application can deal with increases in traffic, high availability is ensuring you can deal with unexpected failures.

I described scaling the number of server instances of your application to meet demand, but running more instances of your application also makes it more highly available. For example, if you are running three instances, and one of those instances unexpectedly crashes, you have two more that are still able to serve traffic.

High availability isn't just about running more servers though, or at least not without some further conditions. While uncommon, it's possible for cloud providers to experience widespread issues on their network. For example, there might be routing or DNS issues in one of their data centers. If your application is hosted exclusively in one data center, such as us-east-1 on AWS, that means your application is going to be unavailable.

To cater for this case, you can deploy to different regions and/or availability zones. For example, you might deploy some instances to a data center on the East Coast of the US, and some to the West Coast of the US. This increases the availability of your service, as should one data center go down, you still have servers in another that can serve traffic.

This does add to your costs and complexity though, as you now need to ensure your servers are running in different regions and/or availability zones, and if you combine that with auto-scaling, you need to ensure you can scale up and down in both regions too.

These cost and complexity considerations are taken care of with serverless. Much like scalability, high availability is just baked into serverless. Because you're not spinning up your own servers, and the cloud provider is handling how and where to host your application, they also take care of ensuring it's highly available.

That's because you're not tied to a specific set of servers, regions, or availability zones. Even if there was a catastrophic failure, and all the data centers in the US went down, your serverless application would simply be served from another country instead. Latency to your end users would increase a little, but that's a small price to pay for maintaining your application's services.

If you want to get an idea of the scale at which Cloudflare operates its network, I recommend checking out https://statusmap.cloudflare.community/. It's a community-maintained project, but it shows you all of the data centers Cloudflare operates, and just how much coverage they provide worldwide. Green dots indicate the data center is available, orange indicates it's undergoing maintenance or is being rerouted to another data center. The following is a snapshot, just to give you an idea:

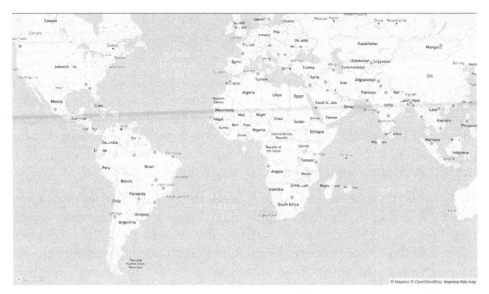

In short, serverless applications built on Cloudflare are global by default.

We've talked a lot about the manual work required for the likes of AWS, which brings us nicely on to the final principle: no server maintenance.

No Server Maintenance

Finally, with serverless, there should never be a need to maintain any servers because with serverless, you don't spin up your own servers. No upgrading the version of the programming language you're using, no upgrading the operating system, nothing like that. If you deploy your application to an EC2 instance, you'll need to upgrade the language version you're using yourself.

You're still responsible for upgrading the dependencies you introduce, such as packages and libraries, but besides that, there should be no dependency or server management whatsoever. If you want to change the version of the language you're using, or even change languages entirely, that should be a painless process and a simple configuration change.

This is one of the primary reasons why I enjoy developing serverless applications. I can focus on what I enjoy most, and that's writing code.

Ready to Go Serverless?

So that's the three-dollar tour of serverless. Now it's time to write some code. As you go through the book, you'll master building serverless applications through hands-on projects. You'll build several different applications to showcase specific serverless concepts.

Should you get stuck at any point or simply want to view the finished projects without making them yourself, you can do so on GitHub.[1] This repository contains all the completed projects.

Let's build some serverless applications!

---

1.   https://github.com/apeacock1991/serverless-apps-on-cloudflare/

## CHAPTER 1

Deploy Your First Cloudflare Worker

Let's jump right in and deploy your first serverless function to Cloudflare. You're going to build an API for storing photos. Over the course of the next five chapters, you will gradually build up the functionality of the API. Here are the steps you'll take:

1. Deploy a simple Worker (you'll do that in this chapter)
2. Update the Worker to include some API endpoints, using in-memory storage for now
3. Explore how you can test a Worker programmatically
4. Replace the in-memory storage with an SQL database
5. Introduce some middleware to provide simple authentication, using Worker-to-Worker calls

By the time you finish Chapter 5, you'll have built all of this. If, like me, you like to see it pictured, here's a simple diagram of what you're building.

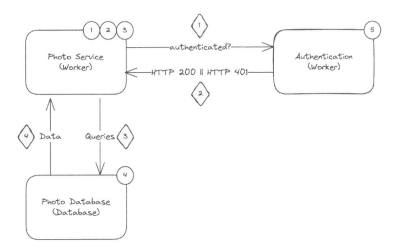

Circled numbers show the new elements introduced in each chapter. Diamond-numbered steps represent the sequence of interactions when the application processes a request.

OK, let's create a Cloudflare Worker.

Create a New Worker

When working on Cloudflare's platform, you'll mainly use their command-line tool (CLI) called Wrangler alongside C3. They do pretty much everything you need when building applications on Cloudflare — creating projects, deploying code, checking serverless app logs and much more.

Right now, you'll use C3 to make what Cloudflare calls a Worker (Azure calls them Functions, AWS calls them Lambdas — different names, same deal: deploying code in a serverless setup). While different cloud providers might have different names for their products, they fundamentally work in the same way.

Cloudflare Workers run on Google Chrome's V8 JavaScript engine, meaning you can use whatever you use in client-side JavaScript. It's important to realize that it's not a Node environment, though it does support a growing number of Node packages via the Node compatibility flag.[1]

In September 2024, Cloudflare released version 2 of their Node compatibility flag—this is now the default version on all new Workers and Pages projects on the latest version of Wrangler. It added significantly more support for Node libraries than was possible on version 1, unlocking far more npm packages for use.

This is achieved with a two pronged approach:

- A subset of Node.js APIs implemented directly in the Workers Runtime

- Polyfills for the majority of other Node.js APIs

In the event a package you want to use relies on an unsupported Node API, you can provide a polyfill yourself, or perhaps there might be one available online.[2] With the addition of version 2, I can see a world where there's full Node support in the not-so-distant future.

---

1. https://developers.cloudflare.com/workers/platform/nodejs-compatibility/
2. https://blog.cloudflare.com/more-npm-packages-on-cloudflare-workers-combining-polyfills-and-native-code/

Language Support

Cloudflare supports more than just JavaScript and TypeScript; any language that compiles to JavaScript is fair game. For example, PHP, F#, Scala, Python, Kotlin, and more.

If you're into WebAssembly (WASM), you're covered too. While WASM language support is expanding, Cloudflare specifically highlights C and Rust as languages that work well on their platform when compiled to WASM.

First-class support for other programming languages is coming too. In April 2024, Cloudflare announced that Python can now be deployed directly to a Worker without the need to compile it to JavaScript or WebAssembly.

For information on other languages and the complete list of what's supported, Cloudflare has an exhaustive list in their docs.

Before you dive in, ensure you have Node.js and Node Package Manager (npm) installed—you'll need at least version 18 of Node. Wrangler relies on them to do its thing.[3]

Once installed, you can create a new project using C3, which is what Cloudflare calls its CLI tool for use with npm create:

```
$ npm create cloudflare@2.21.1 -- --no-auto-update
```

Note: I'll be using the version number of 2.21.1 when creating new projects. When creating your own projects, you can use cloudflare@latest to use the latest version, ensuring you have the latest and greatest features.

You're passing the --no-auto-update flag so that the command behaves consistently with what's documented in the book, as well as ensure the starting code for the projects matches what's in the book. If you run into issues when creating any projects, I recommend removing this flag and trying the latest version.

When you run the command, you'll be prompted to answer a few questions. I suggest you answer as follows:

- Agree to install the create-cloudflare npm module.

- For the directory, you can use whatever you like. I'm going to use photo-service. This will also, by default, be the name of your Worker.

- Select "Hello World" Worker.

---

3.   https://docs.npmjs.com/downloading-and-installing-node-js-and-npm

- Use TypeScript.

- Use Git.

- Lastly, it will ask if you want to deploy your application. For now, opt not to deploy.

After a moment, you should see something like this:

```
$ npm create cloudflare@2.21.1 -- --no-auto-update
Need to install the following packages:
  create-cloudflare@2.21.1
Ok to proceed? (y) y

using create-cloudflare version 2.21.1

Create an application with Cloudflare Step 1 of 3

In which directory do you want to create your application?
dir ./photo-service

What type of application do you want to create?
type "Hello World" Worker

Do you want to use TypeScript?
yes typescript

Copying files from "hello-world" template

Retrieving current workerd compatibility date
compatibility date 2023-10-30

Do you want to use git for version control?
yes git

Application created
```

The script will then install dependencies using npm. You might think workerd is a typo: it's not. It's the name for runtime Cloudflare uses for its Workers.

Although you're using npm create, under the hood a lot of the work is being done by Wrangler. You'll interact more closely with Wrangler throughout the book. In short, it's Cloudflare's Developer Platform command-line interface (CLI), allowing you to manage projects and resources.

That's all there is to creating a new Worker. You could now create a Cloudflare account and run the deploy command, and you'd have your first Worker deployed without any hassle.

For now though, let's see what your options are for configuring that Worker.

Configure a Worker

Let's take a look at a few important files.

First, there's that wrangler.toml. I'd never come across Tom's Obvious Minimal Language (TOML) before, but if you've ever worked with YAML, TOML is doing the same thing, providing a human-friendly format for your application's configuration.

This is where all your Cloudflare-specific configuration for your Worker goes. It's presently pretty bare, but you'll be dressing it up in later chapters. There are four configuration options currently set:

- *name*: the name for your Worker. This value must be url-friendly, so no spaces, but you can use hyphens for separating words.

- *main*: which file is the entry point to your Worker, so when it receives a request, it'll call the fetch function in the file configured here.

- *compatibility_date*: what version of the Worker's runtime to use. Cloudflare recommends periodically updating this date, but you can just leave it, and Cloudflare will support old runtimes forever (their words!).

- *compatibility_flags*: allow you to tweak the runtime environment, and we'll cover this later in the book.

The compatibility date is there because bugs you rely on, either knowingly or unknowingly, might get fixed in newer versions. Cloudflare's platform could undergo backward-incompatible changes, resulting in your application breaking. Check out Cloudflare's documentation for the complete list of such changes.[4]

wrangler.toml is the configuration file you will be changing the most. But two others are worth mentioning:

- *package.json*: used to define the npm packages your Worker depends on

- *tsconfig.json*: used to tweak the TypeScript configuration

That covers the configuration files, so let's look at the code C3 has created to get you started.

---

4.   https://developers.cloudflare.com/workers/platform/compatibility-dates/

Implement Logic in Your Workers

It's time to look at the code that will be executed when your Worker receives a request. All code in the book will be TypeScript, but if types aren't your thing, feel free to use vanilla JavaScript.

All application code for your Workers will be in the src directory, and for now, Cloudflare has created a single file for you. It'll look something like this:

```
export interface Env {
  // MY_KV_NAMESPACE: KVNamespace;
}

export default {
  async fetch(
    request: Request,
    env: Env,
    ctx: ExecutionContext
  ): Promise<Response> {
    return new Response('Hello World!');
  },
};
```

Short and sweet, but this demonstrates something very important: the entry point to every Cloudflare Worker. Each Cloudflare Worker must export a default module, exposing methods that Cloudflare will call when your Worker receives a request.

As you can see, a single fetch function was generated, which is called whenever a HTTP request is received by your Worker. There's also an interface defined for the environment that is used to define some Cloudflare-specific dependencies. You'll be using these throughout the book, with the first one introduced in Chapter 4, Persist Data with D1, on page 33.

The fetch function takes three parameters:

1. *request* represents the HTTP request that was received, and exposes methods that allow you to see the body, headers, and HTTP method. Its type comes from the Fetch API that's built into JavaScript, with Cloudflare adding some extra functionality to it.[5]

2. *env* provides information available in the environment, such as secrets. In later chapters we'll use these to access to other Cloudflare services, such as databases, caches, and queues. (There's information and links to these products in the Env interface defined at the top of the file.)

---

5. https://developer.mozilla.org/en-US/docs/Web/API/Request

3. *ctx* is the execution context, and provides access to a couple of methods that allow you to change the behavior of your Worker. For example, it provides a method called waitUntil that allows you to extend the execution time of your Worker after returning a response. This is particularly handy for returning a response to the client, while still processing something in your Worker.

Lastly, the function has to return a response to the incoming HTTP request. The response is always an instance of the Response class, that once again comes from the Fetch API. For now, the Worker is just returning a piece of text that I'm sure you've seen before.

Organizing Serverless Code

Good programming practices still apply to serverless, with the entry point to your serverless function effectively being the controller, and then incoming requests can be routed by the controller to your application's logic.

For instance, creating a simple API might involve having a serverless function for each endpoint. Imagine /foo and /bar having their own serverless functions, implemented by individual Workers. Alternatively, you could go for a more "monolithic" approach, routing all requests to a single function, which then handles them accordingly.

There's no strict right or wrong here—just trade-offs. Multiple functions allow you to keep each function small and focused, but may lead to code duplication. With multiple functions, it's also a bit trickier to visualize how the functions map to the API structure. On the flip side, a monolithic function reduces duplication and offers a clear API view, but the code might get complex as your API grows. In this chapter, you'll get to see what the monolithic approach looks like.

As a rule of thumb, I'd start with a single function. If things get complicated, you can split it later. Thanks to the ease of deploying serverless functions, making such changes is typically way less costly than breaking up a monolithic container-based app.

Run Scheduled Tasks

Scheduled tasks aren't needed for this project, but Cloudflare lets you define Cron Triggers that execute your Worker based on a schedule. If you need to, you could add a scheduled function to your Worker and set up the schedule using cron syntax. For instance, in your wrangler.toml, you would add this:

```
[triggers]
crons = ["*/15 * * * *"]
```

This would result in the Worker's scheduled function being executed every fifteen minutes. As crons is an array, you can configure a Worker to be executed on different schedules. Here's how you can differentiate between different triggers being executed:

```
export default {
  async scheduled(
    event: ScheduledController,
    env: Env,
    ctx: ExecutionContext
  ) {
    switch (event.cron) {
    // You can set up to three schedules maximum.
    case "*/15 * * * *":
      console.log("This will be executed every 15 minutes");
      break;
    case "*/30 * * * *":
      console.log("This will be executed every 30 minutes");
      break;
    }
  }
}
```

When the scheduled function is triggered, you can see which cron trigger is being executed by looking at event.cron. It's possible to define both a fetch and scheduled function and have your Worker handle HTTP requests and scheduled tasks.

The current Worker does not need to use scheduled tasks, but it's useful to know this functionality is available for the future.

To see the full lifecycle of a Cloudflare Worker, let's deploy this skeleton Worker to Cloudflare.

Deploy Your First Worker

To deploy your Worker to Cloudflare's platform, you'll be using Wrangler.

You'll need a free Cloudflare account before you can deploy anything though, so head over to https://dash.cloudflare.com/signup and create one now.

During registration, it'll ask you what subdomain you want to use when you deploy your applications in development. This subdomain is specific to your Cloudflare account, and will be used for all your projects to make the URLs for your applications unique.

Once you've signed up, go to the root folder of the photo-service folder you created, and run the following:

```
$ npm run deploy
```

Under the hood, this is executing wrangler deploy. As part of the bootstrap of the Worker using C3, Cloudflare added some handy scripts in package.json. If you look at the file, you will see a scripts section. You can run any of them using npm run the-script-name.

The first time you run this command, you'll need to jump through some hoops to authenticate with Cloudflare. A new browser tab should open, requesting you sign in to Cloudflare. Sign in and grant any permissions requested. Once that's complete, you can return to your terminal, and you should see your Worker deploying.

Sometimes, the authentication step times out, so if after you've logged in, your terminal is waiting for a command to be entered, just run the npm run deploy command again.

You won't need to do this for subsequent deploys, as Cloudflare will store your authentication tokens locally on your device, but you may need to periodically sign in if they expire.

Once you're authenticated, and Wrangler deploys your Worker, you should see something like this:

```
$ wrangler deploy
wrangler 3.15.0
-------------------

Total Upload: 0.19 KiB / gzip: 0.16 KiB
Uploaded photo-service (1.74 sec)
Published photo-service (5.97 sec)
  https://photo-service.your-cloudflare-subdomain.workers.dev
Current Deployment ID: 00ca0bb5-25d0-4699-9919-99be668b2b0a
```

It'll show you the total size of your Worker and output the URL where your Worker is hosted. By default, Cloudflare will upload your Worker to a subdomain it provides. It usually follows the format of {worker-name}.{your-cloudflare-subdomain}.workers.dev. You can change the your-cloudflare-subdomain part in your Cloudflare Dashboard, under the Workers tab on the left menu.

Cloudflare handles everything necessary to expose a Worker, including the DNS for this subdomain, along with any SSL certificates. You can copy the URL that's output, put it in your browser, and you'll see the following:

Hello World!

It may take a few minutes for the DNS to update for your new Worker, so you may see errors initially, but typically it's available instantly.

Worker Limits

As with most platforms, there are limits to keep in mind when building Workers. One of the main ones is the size of your Worker. There's a 1MB limit on the free plan, and a 10MB limit on the paid plan, which currently costs $5/month.

There's a limit to the number of Workers you can create: 100 with the free plan and 500 with the paid. I've yet to hit these limits, but you can contact Cloudflare to increase some of the limits if needed.

What You've Learned

That rounds out the first chapter, and you've already managed to deploy your first serverless application, even if it's a very small one.

In this chapter, you learned how to build a simple serverless function and deploy it to Cloudflare. You also learned the languages you can use on Cloudflare's platform, and used your first commands from C3 and Wrangler.

In the next chapter, you're going to build out the functionality of this Worker by adding endpoints to create an API.

## CHAPTER 2

Build a Serverless API

In the previous chapter, you got a glimpse of how to deploy serverless applications on Cloudflare. Right now, you have a single photo service Worker up and running, but it doesn't provide any photo services—it just responds to HTTP requests with "Hello World."

Now let's kick things up a notch, and make your photo service Worker into an API that provides specific functionality to users.

The Worker you build will be the foundation for your photo API. This Worker will serve a few endpoints for dealing with images, so you need to add these three endpoints:

1. *GET /images* will return all the images the service holds, optionally supporting a count parameter to limit the results.

2. *GET /images/:id* will return the image with the given ID.

3. *POST /images* will create a new image.

In this chapter, you'll tackle those three routes and set up the necessary logic to make them work. Down the road, you'll bring in some dependencies for the Worker, like connecting to a database for persistence. But for now, we're keeping it simple and handling everything in memory.

Let's implement some logic!

Route HTTP Requests

To handle various endpoints and HTTP methods, you need to be able to execute requests against the correct logic in the Worker. In the last chapter, when you deployed the Worker, you hit the root of the site (https://photo-service.your-cloudflare-subdomain.workers.dev). There was no path in the URL.

If you were to take the URL that Wrangler returned when you deployed that Worker, and add any path to the end of it (such as https://photo-...-workers.dev/test) you'd see the exact same response.

Cloudflare links a Worker to a domain by default, routing all requests to the domain that's associated with that Worker. For now, we're using Cloudflare's workers.dev domain for easy development. When you deploy a Worker in development, the name of your Worker plus the subdomain associated with your Cloudflare account will be used to create the full URL that routes to your Worker's code.

Later in the book, we'll add custom domains and route them to a Worker.

For now, you're going to use a handy npm package called itty-router, a compact router that helps you route requests based on the path and method in the HTTP request. To add it to the Worker's dependencies, run this command:

```
$ npm install itty-router --save
```

This will install the package and add it to your package.json.

Next, you need to import itty-router and configure the first route by replacing the contents of src/index.ts with:

```typescript
import { Router } from 'itty-router'

const router = Router()

router.get('/images', getImages)
  .get('*', () => new Response('Not found', { status: 404 }));

export interface Env {
  // MY_KV_NAMESPACE: KVNamespace;
}

export default {
  async fetch(
    request: Request,
    env: Env,
    ctx: ExecutionContext
  ): Promise<Response> {
    return router.fetch(request);
  },
};
```

In only five lines of code, you have configured the router to route any requests to /images to a yet-to-be-defined handler called getImages. You can add any type of HTTP method and path, and either direct it to call a function or implement the logic inline.

Check out the inline handling in the next line, where the wildcard selector catches any requests that don't match a defined route. In this scenario, a 404 will be returned, indicating that no handler was found for the incoming HTTP request. The router executes the first matching handler, so place the wildcard last to treat 404 handling as a last resort.

You can use wildcards when defining paths too: You could define a wildcard for a given path:

```
router.get('/images/*', allImageHandler)
```

This would catch any paths that start with /images, for example:

- /images/1
- /images/foo
- /images/foo/bar

This shows you the simplicity and power of itty-router, which has many more features in such a small package, such as query string parsing and middleware. You'll meet 'itty-router' again later, but feel free to check out the documentation in the meantime.[1]

The last step to actually route a request to a handler is to execute the router in the fetch method, which is just as simple as defining the routes themselves:

```
export default {
  async fetch(
    request: Request,
    env: Env,
    ctx: ExecutionContext
  ): Promise<Response> {
    return router.fetch(request);
  },
};
```

Simply invoke the fetch method on the configured router, passing the request as a parameter. The router will use the request to figure out which handler to execute. Just a quick reminder, the request parameter passed to fetch is an instance of a modified version of the Fetch API's Request class.

That's the routing done, and although you don't have a handler defined yet for GET /images, you can run the Worker to check it's behaving as you'd expect.

Let's talk about running Workers locally.

---

1.   https://github.com/kwhitley/itty-router

Locally Test Workers

Previously, you tested a Worker by deploying it to Cloudflare, which is fine during development. However, once your application is live and customers are using it, you'll need a safer way to test changes. You probably don't want to impact your production data by testing in production, and having to deploy each time would be incredibly slow in comparison to being able to test changes locally.

Typically, local development introduces a mismatch between production and your local environment. While the data won't be the same, Cloudflare simulates the production environment locally. For an even more realistic setup, you can push your Worker to a remote sandbox environment by turning off local mode—something we'll cover shortly.

To run a worker locally, simply run the following command:

```
$ npm run dev
```

Under the hood, this is executing wrangler dev. After a few seconds, you'll see some output like this:

```
wrangler 3.15.0
-------------------------------------------------------
[ERROR] service core:user:photo-service: Uncaught ReferenceError:
  getImages is not defined
  at null.<anonymous> (index.js:74:23)

[ERROR] MiniflareCoreError [ERR_RUNTIME_FAILURE]:
The Workers runtime failed to start.
There is likely additional logging output above.

Listening at http://0.0.0.0:8787
- http://127.0.0.1:8787
- http://192.168.1.90:8787
Total Upload: 0.19 KiB / gzip: 0.16 KiB

[b] browser, [d] Devtools, [l] turn off local mode, [c] clear [x] exit
```

As you can see from the output, your Worker has been started, but errors have been reported in the console. Keep in mind the port may vary.

There are a few options available. You can try each of them:

1. *b* will open the browser, making a GET request to the root URL of your Worker

2. *d* will open dev tools, allowing you to debug your Worker more easily using Chrome's dev tools

3. *l* turns off local mode, which means your Worker will run in a remote sandbox environment on Cloudflare's network

4. *c* clears the console and *x* stops your Worker running

It's pretty awesome to be able to run your code in a production-like environment in seconds, either locally or remotely. If you want to run a Worker remotely, in a sandbox environment on Cloudflare's actual network, you can start a Worker with `npm run dev -- --remote`.

If you need to pass parameters to an npm script, you do so by inserting `--` followed by any parameters. This is a common convention used by many command-line tools to separate the script itself from any parameters.

The error you see is exactly what you would expect, as you haven't implemented `getImages` yet, so let's do that now.

Windows Compatibility

The majority of the Cloudflare tooling will work on Windows, but some third-party libraries that they rely on aren't supported, so you may experience some issues; you'll see errors in the terminal when you run commands. If you experience significant problems, I'd recommend running the commands in a Linux VM, or making use of Windows Subsystem for Linux (WSL).

Define HTTP Handlers

For each route you configure, you need to define a handler, which is responsible for handling any HTTP requests sent to it.

As you're implementing the endpoint to return all the images, you need some dummy data to return. Create a new folder under src called data, and a new file within data called image_store.ts:

```
export const ALL_IMAGES = [
  {
    id: 3,
    url: 'https://bar.com/img1',
    author: 'Lara Lobster'
  },
  {
    id: 2,
    url: 'https://baz.com/img2',
    author: 'Larry Lobster'
  },
  {
    id: 1,
```

```
    url: 'https://foo.com/img1',
    author: 'Bart Simpson'
  }
]
```

There's nothing fancy going on here; you're simply defining a constant that contains an array of dummy images and some metadata. When you get to Chapter 4, Persist Data with D1, on page 33, you'll remove this file in favor of persisting data to a database.

Next, you need to create a new folder at src/handlers and create a new file named get_images.ts inside of the handlers folder. To keep the Worker's code tidy, the handlers will be stored in a separate folder. In src/handlers/get_images.ts, insert the following code:

```
import { ALL_IMAGES } from "../data/image_store";
import { IRequest } from 'itty-router'

const getImages = (request: IRequest) => {
  let images = ALL_IMAGES

  if (request.query.count) {
    images = images.slice(0, parseInt(request.query.count[0]))
  }

  return new Response(JSON.stringify(images), {
    headers: { 'content-type': 'application/json' }
  });
};

export default getImages;
```

Let's step through the code to understand what's going on.

First, there are a couple of imports, the first being the dummy data, the second importing the IRequest type from itty-router.

Second, a constant is defined named getImages, that contains an arrow function. The parameters for that function are defined in the parentheses, and the function's logic is defined between the curly braces. In this case, there's one parameter, which is the HTTP request.

Next, all the images defined in src/data/image_store.ts are stored in a variable to manipulate later. If the request has a count query string parameter, that is used to reduce the number of results returned.

Finally, the response is returned as JSON. You must always return an instance of the Response class. When creating a response, the first argument is the response body, and the second is any metadata in the response such as status code and headers.

That's all there is to it: a pretty simple function that will return all the images.

Before you can test the Worker, you need to make one more small change, and that's in src/index.ts. All you need to do is import the new function, so the router has access to it. Open up src/index.ts and add the following import alongside the other imports at the top:

```
import getImages from './handlers/get_images'
```

You can now run npm run dev and hit the /images route of your Worker, and you should see some JSON returned.

You can also see any requests hitting your Worker in the console too, including the path and status code returned.

That's the basic flow of adding any endpoint in a Worker. However, the API is not yet complete, so let's add the next endpoint.

Create Resources Using HTTP POST

The endpoint you just added was a GET endpoint, which is usually used to retrieve data. Alongside retrieving data, an application regularly needs to create data. One way to create data in an API is using a POST request. Let's add in the POST /images endpoint, which will create an image.

As before, you're first going to add in the routing for the new endpoint. You do that in src/index.ts, updating the routing logic near the top of the file:

```
router.get('/images', getImages)
    .post('/images', createImage)
    .get('*', () => new Response('Not found', { status: 404 }));
```

This is very similar to the code you added to handle GET /images, except you use .post instead of .get. This will route any POST requests to /images to the yet-to-be-defined createImage handler.

To define the handler, create a new file at src/handlers/create_image.ts and add the following code:

```
import { ALL_IMAGES } from "../data/image_store";
import { IRequest } from 'itty-router'

const createImage = async(request: IRequest) => {
  const imageRequest = await request.json()
  const newImage = {
    id: parseInt(imageRequest.id),
    url: imageRequest.url,
    author: imageRequest.author
  }
```

```
  ALL_IMAGES.unshift(newImage)

  return new Response(JSON.stringify(newImage), {
    status: 201,
    headers: { 'content-type': 'application/json' }
  });
}
export default createImage;
```

The code is relatively straightforward, but let's step through the code section by section:

First, there are some imports, the same ones as in the other handler. Then, a function called createImage is defined, which accepts the HTTP request passed through by itty-router. Note that this time, we define an asynchronous function, as you need to call asynchronous methods within the function. When an asynchronous function is defined with async, it returns a Promise. Behind the scenes, itty-router will handle resolving the Promise.

Next, the first line of the function parses the body of the HTTP request as JSON, and returns a Promise containing an object representing the JSON in the request. await is used as the json method is asynchronous, and you want to get the value from the Promise it returns.

After you have the request as an object, you create a new object representing the new image you want to create. You can then add the new image to the existing list of images stored in the ALL_IMAGES array. unshift is used to add the new image to the beginning of the array, just so that the latest image is first in the list.

Finally, a response is returned that will be used by itty-router to respond to the initial HTTP request. Alongside the response body, you can adjust the response's status code and headers.

Before you test the POST endpoint, you need to import the createImage function in src/index.ts along with the other imports:

```
import createImage from './handlers/create_image';
```

Start your Worker again using npm run dev, and run the following command to send a POST request to the new endpoint:

```
$ curl --data \
  '{ "id": 4, "url": "https://example.com/some_image.png", "author": "Lia" }' \
  -H 'Content-Type: application/json' http://0.0.0.0:8787/images
```

You will see a response like this:

```
{
    "id": 4,
    "url": "https://example.com/some_image.png",
    "author": "Lia"
},
```

The machine-optimized response will differ as it removes all whitespace. The data from the POST request has been utilized to add a new image to the list. To confirm, send a request to GET /images, and the image should appear in the returned list. Keep in mind that since you're storing data in-memory, it resets with each Worker restart.

If you like, you can use a tool like Postman to interact with the API. It's a UI-based option for those who prefer it over the command line.

That's it for the POST endpoint, and you just have one more endpoint to add.

Define Routes with Parameters

In the previous two endpoints, requests always target the same URL. APIs often need to accept parameters in the URL. For this API, you'll need to be able to fetch a single image at a time.

You currently have GET /images, which will return all images, but you can return a single image by passing the ID of an image as a path parameter. The request will then look something like GET /images/1, if you want to get the image with an ID of 1.

Adding this endpoint is very similar to the two you've already added, and you start by adding the new endpoint into the routing configuration in src/index.ts:

```
router.get('/images', getImages)
    .get('/images/:id', getSingleImage)
    .post('/images', createImage)
    .get('*', () => new Response('Not found', { status: 404 }));
```

As before, you've added a single line for the new endpoint. In itty-router, you can pass parameters in a URL by prepending a segment of the URL with a colon. You can add as many parameters as you like: they'll be passed in the request object to your handler, as you'll see next.

With the route configuration added, you can define the handler in src/handlers/get_single_image.ts, shown on the next page.

```
import { ALL_IMAGES } from "../data/image_store";
import { IRequest } from 'itty-router'

const getSingleImage = (request: IRequest) => {
  let image = ALL_IMAGES.find(i => i.id.toString() == request.params.id)

  if (!image) {
    return new Response('Not found', { status: 404 })
  }

  return new Response(JSON.stringify(image), {
    headers: { 'content-type': 'application/json' }
  });
};

export default getSingleImage;
```

There isn't much new here, but you should notice the following line:

```
let image = ALL_IMAGES.find(i => i.id.toString() == request.params.id)
```

This provides the key functionality for the handler, as it attempts to find an image matching the ID passed in the URL. Any parameters in the URL are passed in request.params.

To find the image requested, you use the find method of Array, which allows you to specify a callback to define the logic used to find. When the find is executed, it will loop through every entry in the array until one matches the logic in the callback. If nothing matches, it will return undefined.

Casting each ID in the array to a string is a little wasteful, but as you'll be replacing the static images array later with a database, it's not a concern.

Finally, you import the getSingleImage handler in src/index.ts:

```
import getSingleImage from './handlers/get_single_image';
```

To check the final endpoint is working, start your Worker with npm run dev and go to http://0.0.0.0:8787/images/1 in your browser and you'll see the following response:

```
{"id":1,"url":"https://foo.com/img1","author":"Bart Simpson"}
```

That's all the code needed for the three endpoints; you can verify everything is working in production by deploying using npm run deploy.

Let's recap what was covered in this chapter.

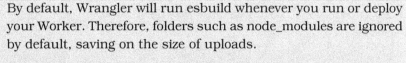

Customizing Builds

By default, Wrangler will run esbuild whenever you run or deploy your Worker. Therefore, folders such as node_modules are ignored by default, saving on the size of uploads.

You may, however, want to run bespoke build steps before your Worker is run or published, such as generating images or documentation.[2]

What You've Learned

You now have three HTTP endpoints in a Cloudflare Worker accepting requests and returning responses. You learned how to define and implement handlers for routes using itty-router. You are now able to define both GET and POST requests, as well as define routes with parameters. And you learned how to test your Worker locally without deploying it to production using npm run dev.

So far, you've been testing the endpoints manually. In the next chapter, you'll learn how you can test Workers using automated testing.

---

2.   https://developers.cloudflare.com/workers/wrangler/custom-builds/

## CHAPTER 3

Run Tests Against a Worker

Your photo API is taking shape, with three endpoints now implemented, allowing it to retrieve and store images. So far, you've been running the Worker locally, and manually testing it by hitting it with HTTP requests, which is great for quick development.

But as the app grows, you'll need a better way to ensure the Worker behaves right. You want confidence that changes, like new features or bug fixes, won't unexpectedly mess things up before going into production.

To do that, you're going to write some end-to-end tests for the API.

For end-to-end tests against a Cloudflare Worker, I recommend using Vitest. You can go with any framework you like—I like using Vitest, and it's the library that is included by default when you create a new Worker with npm create cloudflare.

This comes with some benefits, as Cloudflare has worked closely with Vitest to ensure that when your tests run, they run in the actual Cloudflare runtime called workerd. This ensures that the test environment is as production-like as possible.

Let's jump right in.

Define the Test Setup

Before diving into adding and running a test, we need to define the test setup. Cloudflare has already created a folder to house your tests in, named test, and created a new file in that new folder called index.spec.ts. This file, shown on the next page, contains the basics needed to run a test against your Worker:

```
import {
  env,
  createExecutionContext,
  waitOnExecutionContext,
  SELF
} from "cloudflare:test";
import { describe, it, expect } from "vitest";
import worker from "../src/index";

// For now, you'll need to do something like this to get a correctly-typed
// `Request` to pass to `worker.fetch()`.
const IncomingRequest = Request<unknown, IncomingRequestCfProperties>;

describe("Hello World worker", () => {
  it("responds with Hello World! (unit style)", async () => {
    const request = new IncomingRequest("http://example.com");

    // Create an empty context to pass to `worker.fetch()`.
    const ctx = createExecutionContext();
    const response = await worker.fetch(request, env, ctx);

    // Wait for all `Promise`s passed to `ctx.waitUntil()`
    // to settle before running test assertions
    await waitOnExecutionContext(ctx);

    expect(await response.text()).toMatchInlineSnapshot(`"Hello World!"`);
  });

  it("responds with Hello World! (integration style)", async () => {
    const response = await SELF.fetch("https://example.com");
    expect(await response.text()).toMatchInlineSnapshot(`"Hello World!"`);
  });
});
```

There's quite a lot going in only a few lines of code, so let's break it down.

First, several dependencies are imported that are needed to run the tests:

```
import {
  env,
  createExecutionContext,
  waitOnExecutionContext,
  SELF
} from "cloudflare:test";
import { describe, it, expect } from "vitest";
import worker from "../src/index";
```

A number of constants are imported from cloudflare:test, which are made available from the npm package @cloudflare/vitest-pool-workers. The first three are needed to write unit tests against Cloudflare Workers, as they provide the necessary parameters and handling for the fetch function of your Worker. SELF is needed to run integration tests, as you'll see shortly.

Lastly for the imports, there are some functions needed from Vitest that you'll be using to write the tests, along with an import for your Worker. If you've ever written tests before, you'll be familiar with the names of the constants imported from vitest, as they are pretty standard across most test frameworks.

After the imports comes the test setup itself:

```
// For now, you'll need to do something like this to get a correctly-typed
// `Request` to pass to `worker.fetch()`.
const IncomingRequest = Request<unknown, IncomingRequestCfProperties>;

describe("Hello World worker", () => {
  it("responds with Hello World! (unit style)", async () => {
    const request = new IncomingRequest("http://example.com");

    // Create an empty context to pass to `worker.fetch()`.
    const ctx = createExecutionContext();
    const response = await worker.fetch(request, env, ctx);

    // Wait for all `Promise`s passed to `ctx.waitUntil()`
    // to settle before running test assertions
    await waitOnExecutionContext(ctx);

    expect(await response.text()).toMatchInlineSnapshot(`"Hello World!"`);
  });

  it("responds with Hello World! (integration style)", async () => {
    const response = await SELF.fetch("https://example.com");
    expect(await response.text()).toMatchInlineSnapshot(`"Hello World!"`);
  });
});
```

Similarly to most test frameworks, you wrap a series of tests in a describe block, followed by the actual tests themselves. When the project was created, Cloudflare created two example tests. The first is a unit test:

```
it("responds with Hello World! (unit style)", async () => {
  const request = new IncomingRequest("http://example.com");

  // Create an empty context to pass to `worker.fetch()`.
  const ctx = createExecutionContext();
  const response = await worker.fetch(request, env, ctx);

  // Wait for all `Promise`s passed to `ctx.waitUntil()`
  // to settle before running test assertions
  await waitOnExecutionContext(ctx);

  expect(await response.text()).toMatchInlineSnapshot(`"Hello World!"`);
});
```

As this is a unit test, all the parameters have to be created before you can call your Worker. A fake request is created as well as the execution context that's passed to every invocation of your Worker. You can then call your

Worker, passing these parameters, and then create any assertions you wish based on the response. If your Worker had dependencies, you could mock and stub objects in similar ways to other test frameworks.

The second example is an integration test:

```
it("responds with Hello World! (integration style)", async () => {
  const response = await SELF.fetch("https://example.com");
  expect(await response.text()).toMatchInlineSnapshot(`"Hello World!"`);
});
```

This is the format you'll use to write your tests in this chapter. It's a lot more concise because you don't need to create the parameters. This is because it simulates how your Worker would be executed in production, including the same runtime, where it simply receives an HTTP request. To run against that runtime, all you need to do is call SELF.fetch, and then assert against the response.

One key thing to note is that when you call the Worker using SELF.fetch, you need to pass a fully-valid URL. As the tests against your Worker are going to be executed in the same runtime as production, it would expect a fully-qualified domain to be passed. You can use whatever domain you like.

There's just one optional change to make to this file, updating the describe block to reflect your Worker, like so:

```
describe("Photo Service", () => {
```

With the setup complete, you can write your first test.

Write a Test for 404s

Now that you understand the test setup, let's dive into writing tests. You'll start by adding a test to ensure that the Worker returns a 404 error when a non-existent endpoint is called. It's a straightforward test to kick things off. Here's the necessary code:

```
describe("Photo service", () => {
  it("returns a 404 if a non-existent endpoint is called", async () => {
    const response = await SELF.fetch(
      'http://www.example.com/invalid-endpoint'
    );
    expect(response.status).toEqual(404);
  });
});
```

Make sure you remove any existing it conditions that Cloudflare had already created.

You define a test using it in Vitest, with the first parameter providing the description for the test case and the second defining a callback where you write the test's logic.

Within that callback, you first call the Worker, and provide an invalid path in the request. By default, a GET request is made, and fetch will return a Response object, providing all the standard HTTP methods you'd expect, such as the status and any headers.

Finally, you define the expectation for this test case by simply asserting that the response's status code is returned as 404.

With the test written, let's run the test file to see what happens. When Wrangler created the Worker, a number of helpful npm scripts were created too. One of them allows us to run tests using Vitest:

```
$ npm run test
```

This will produce output that looks something like this:

```
> photo-service@0.0.0 test
> vitest run

 RUN  v0.31.0

 ✓ test/index.spec.ts (1)
   ✓ Photo Service (1)
     ✓ returns a 404 if a non-existent endpoint is called

 Test Files  1 passed (1)
      Tests  1 passed (1)
   Start at  06:22:49
   Duration  931ms
```

As per the output, a single test was found and executed, and most importantly, it passed.

You can now continue adding tests for the other endpoints.

Write Tests for GET /images

Now that you've wrapped up a test for returning a 404, it's time to move on to tests for the defined endpoints. The format will remain quite consistent across tests, as you'll essentially apply the same formula for each one:

1. Make an HTTP request to a Worker
2. Write expectations against the returned response

The data fed into the request and the expectations you write, will vary per test, but for the most part, they'll look very similar.

Ensure you cover every endpoint with at least one test, and think about testing every possible permutation. This involves exploring the parameters applicable to each endpoint and crafting a test for each parameter. Additionally, if an endpoint involves branching logic, test all possible code paths.

If you take the GET /images endpoint as the first endpoint to write tests for, you need to test that:

1. It returns an HTTP 200 status code

2. It returns a set of images in the body

3. If the count parameter is provided, it should limit the results in the body to that number

As the first one is very similar to the test case you wrote, let's tackle that first. Below the previous test, add the following:

```
describe("GET /images", () => {
  it("returns a 200 OK response", async () => {
    const response = await SELF.fetch('http://www.example.com/images');
    expect(response.status).toEqual(200);
  });
});
```

There's not much to go over here, as it's essentially the same as the previous, except the request you're making is to a real endpoint, and the response code you expect back should be a 200, which indicates a successful response.

To organize your tests effectively, consider nesting describe blocks inside one another. The top-level describe is for the the photo service as a whole, and within that, you should use additional describe blocks to further specify the focus of a particular test. For instance, if you're adding tests for the GET /images endpoint, the describe block should reflect that.

This approach eliminates the need to describe the endpoint for each test case, making it easier to debug failed tests by quickly identifying the problematic endpoint.

You can see the difference this makes if you run the tests again, using npm run test, and note how the test you've just written is now indented in the response, and nested under the describe block you added:

```
✓ test/index.spec.ts (2)
   ✓ Photo Service (2)
     ✓ returns a 404 if a non-existent endpoint is called
     ✓ GET /images (1)
        ✓ returns a 200 OK response

 Test Files  1 passed (1)
      Tests  2 passed (2)
   Start at  06:27:07
   Duration  745ms
```

That's the first test for GET /images, which ensures the correct status code is returned. Let's add a test to validate the response is in the format expected using the following code:

```
describe("GET /images", () => {
  it("should return a 200 OK response", async () => {
    const response = await SELF.fetch('http://www.example.com/images');

    expect(response.status).toEqual(200);
  });

  it("should return images in the response", async () => {
    const response = await SELF.fetch('http://www.example.com/images');
    const json = await response.json();

    expect(json).toEqual(
      expect.arrayContaining([
        expect.objectContaining(
          { id: 3, url: 'https://bar.com/img1',
          author: 'Lara Lobster'}
        )
      ])
    );
  });
});
```

This test is a little more involved, as you're making assertions against the response returned from the API. You're going to use the static data defined in the API in your tests too.

The test setup simply makes a call to GET /images once again, and the response's JSON is parsed into an object.

You can now make assertions on that object, which can be a little tricky. You could just assert against the entire response, but that would make the test quite long. Instead, you're going to assert that the response contains an array, which contains an object matching one of the images in the static data.

Vitest provides a wide range of ways to write assertions using expect.[1] Here, you're using expect.arrayContaining and expect.objectContaining to ensure the response is an array which contains the object expected.

Once again, run the tests using npm run test and make sure they are passing.

Finally, for this endpoint, you want to write a test to ensure that if the count parameter is passed in the query string, the API limits the results. You can do that with the following test, adding it to the GET /images describe block:

```
it("should return a set number of images if count is provided", async () => {
  const response = await SELF.fetch('http://www.example.com/images?count=2');

  const json = await response.json();

  expect(json).toHaveLength(2);
});
```

In this test, you include ?count=2 in the request to restrict the number of returned images. As before, parse the response into an object and use Vitest's toHaveLength expectation to assert that the response comprises two images. The toHaveLength function can be used on any object with a .length property.

If you run the tests once more, you'll see you now have four tests passing.

That covers the tests for the GET /images endpoint, so let's write some for the POST /images endpoint next.

Test POST /images

There's not much difference here between the tests for the GET and POST, but it's worth looking at POST to see how you pass test data when you call the test Worker.

You're going to add a new describe block for the POST endpoint, and add two tests to it. The first will cover checking the status code, and the second will cover the response back from the endpoint.

Here are both tests, which you should add to src/tests/index.test.ts:

```
describe("POST /images", () => {
  it("should return a 201 response code", async() => {
    const payload = {
      "id": 4,
      "url": "https://example.com/some_image.png",
      "author": "Lia"
    };
```

---

1. https://vitest.dev/api/expect.html

```
    const response = await SELF.fetch('http://www.example.com/images', {
      method: "POST",
      body: JSON.stringify(payload)
    });

    expect(response.status).toEqual(201);

  });

  it("should return the created image in the response", async() => {
    const newImage = {
      "id": 4,
      "url": "https://example.com/some_image.png",
      "author": "Lia"
    }

    const response = await SELF.fetch('http://www.example.com/images', {
      method: "POST",
      body: JSON.stringify(newImage)
    });

    const json = await response.json()

    expect(json).toEqual(
      expect.objectContaining(
        newImage
      )
    );
  });
});
```

Most of this should look familiar to you, as you just worked through similar-looking tests for the GET endpoint.

A new describe block has been added, so any tests you write are scoped to that endpoint. The assertions in both are almost identical to the GET endpoint, except that a 201 response is expected for the POST endpoint.

The one part I wanted to highlight was when calling the Worker:

```
const payload = {
  "id": 4,
  "url": "https://example.com/some_image.png",
  "author": "Lia"
};
const response = await SELF.fetch('http://www.example.com/images', {
  method: "POST",
  body: JSON.stringify(payload)
});
```

While calling the GET endpoint allows you to simply provide the path for the request and rely on defaults, a POST request requires additional parameters when using fetch. You can include typical HTTP request components like the body and headers.

In this instance, supply an object as the second parameter to fetch, specifying the method as POST and passing the desired image for creation in JSON format.

Execute the tests once more with npm run test, and you should see all six tests passing.

There's one endpoint currently untested, and that's the endpoint to retrieve a single image. We're not going to write tests for that because the tests are very similar to the endpoint that returns a list of images that you already wrote tests for.

However, if you want to have a go at writing some tests, that would be the perfect opportunity to do so, to practice what you've learned.

What You've Learned

In this chapter, we covered some of the different types of tests you can write. You picked up some Cloudflare-specific knowledge regarding integration tests. And you wrote the tests using Vitest, a quick and simple testing framework.

Up until now, you've been using static data to build the API. However, in a real application, you'll need to be able to store data provided by users. To do so, you'll learn how to use a database with a Worker in the next chapter.

## CHAPTER 4

Persist Data with D1

The Photo API is now fully featured with endpoints, but it's using in-memory storage. That means whenever the Worker is restarted locally, or a new instance of your Worker is created in production, the data is reset to the base state stored in the code.

That's a good setup for getting the hang of Cloudflare Workers, but it won't cut it in a real-world application. In this chapter, you're going to step it up by getting the Worker to talk to a database, removing the in-memory storage in the process.

Cloudflare offers some cool services for storing data outside of a Worker. Later on, you'll dive into caches in Chapter 8, Cache Data with KV, on page 97. And in Chapter 9, Upload and Store Files on R2, on page 113, you'll use R2 for object storage. But for now, let's focus on D1.

D1 is a slick, fully serverless SQL database, built on top of SQLite. It's a perfect match, considering SQLite embraced the term "serverless" long before it became a buzzword in the cloud world.[1]

D1 has all the bells and whistles you'd expect from an SQL database—tables, indexes, keys, backups, and a cool feature to query JSON stored in columns. You can take it up a notch by extracting data from a JSON-stored column and creating new columns on the fly—either at runtime or when you insert a new row.

---

1. https://www.sqlite.org/serverless.html

D1 Pricing

As of now, D1 comes bundled in Cloudflare's free plan. With that, you're looking at 5 million reads a day, 100,000 writes a day, and a storage cap of 5GB. Now, if you decide to upgrade to the $5/month Workers Paid subscription, there are some serious upgrades—25 billion reads daily and 50 million writes. Anything beyond that, and you pay as you go: $0.001 per million rows read, $1.00 per million rows written, and $0.75 per GB stored beyond 5GB.

Create a D1 Database

To start your database persistence journey with a Worker, you'll first create the database. At the time of writing, your D1 database is created in a single location. In the near future, Cloudflare will release read replicas for D1, which cuts down query latency—especially handy when your app gets traffic from different corners of the world.

Creating a database is simple to do using Wrangler:

```
$ npx wrangler d1 create photo-service
```

The last argument is the name of the database. Execute the command above, and you'll see an output similar to this:

```
Successfully created DB 'photo-service'!
```

Add the following to your `wrangler.toml` to connect to it from a Worker:

```
[[ d1_databases ]]
binding = "DB" # i.e. available in your Worker on env.DB
database_name = "photo-service"
database_id = "276bd070-ced5-4552-8d4a-07a151764713"
```

Wrangler has created the database for you and even told you how you can connect a Worker to a D1 database. You'll notice you have just created a single database and might wonder how you separate data between environments, such as development, staging, and production. We'll cover that in Chapter 15, Deploy to Production, on page 213.

Although you've created a resource using Wrangler, there's no need to create a server to house that database or anything like that. As you're operating in a serverless environment, all you need to create is a database, and Cloudflare handles the rest.

Now that you've created a database, you can allow a Worker to access that database using a binding.

Adjusting Database Location

By default, the database will be created in the region closest to where the creation command was issued. However, you may be developing an application in the United Kingdom but for the US market, in which case, you probably want the database to be located in the US.

When creating a database, you can pass –location=wnam to the command to change the location the leader is located in. The current locations to choose from are wnam (Western North America), enam (Eastern North America), weur (Western Europe), eeur (Eastern Europe), and apac (Asia-Pacific)

At present, this means D1 databases are held in a single location. Cloudflare announced in April 2024 that read replication, with your D1 databases globally distributed, is being actively worked on.

Connect a Database to a Worker

You've got this slick SQLite database, but your app code is stuck on the outside looking in. In the old-school way, you'd be looking for a library, juggling credentials, and doing a tightrope act to store them securely.

With Cloudflare, things are a lot different, and for the better. No library hunting, no credential headaches. When connecting your Worker to a database, or any other Cloudflare resource, all you need is a binding.

What's a binding, you ask? It's the mechanism that ties a Worker to a resource. Feel free to create as many bindings as you need—throw in a couple of databases, maybe toss in a cache or two. It's all fair game for a single Worker.

Any bindings for a Worker are configured using the wrangler.toml in your project's root. To connect the existing Worker with the newly-created D1 database, add the following to the bottom of your wrangler.toml:

```
[[ d1_databases ]]
binding = "DB" # i.e. available in your Worker on env.DB
database_name = "photo-service"
database_id = "276bd070-ced5-4552-8d4a-07a151764713"
```

Make sure you replace database_name with the name you used in the d1 create command, if you opted for a different name, and replace the database_id with the ID output after you run the create command. To keep things simple, you can just copy and paste the output from the command into the bottom of wrangler.toml.

The only other parameter to cover above is the binding. This is incredibly important, as this name will be used in your application code to execute queries against a D1 database.

If you want to bind multiple databases to a Worker, you can simply create multiple [[d1_databases]] entries.

Before you can execute queries, tables need to be created to store the data in. To do that, you can use D1 migrations, which we'll cover next.

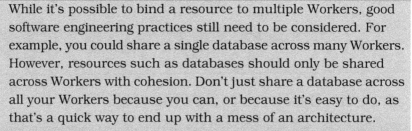

Sharing Bindings Between Workers

While it's possible to bind a resource to multiple Workers, good software engineering practices still need to be considered. For example, you could share a single database across many Workers. However, resources such as databases should only be shared across Workers with cohesion. Don't just share a database across all your Workers because you can, or because it's easy to do, as that's a quick way to end up with a mess of an architecture.

If a single service or API is made up of many Workers, sharing resources between those Workers might make sense. It would likely make less sense if you shared that database across every single Worker within your organization.

Create a Migration

In D1, the primary storage medium is a table. Powered by SQLite, it stores all your app's data neatly in tables. It has everything you'd expect: foreign keys, primary keys, indexes—everything you're used to from a database.

In the early days of my engineering career, keeping tabs on the database state was a headache. SQL scripts, if you were lucky, got committed to version control, and you had to manually apply them to your dev database. It was error-prone, to say the least.

Fast forward to now, and most frameworks come to the rescue. If you're familiar with Ruby on Rails, it gives you migrations to manage a database's schema and state. D1 does likewise, with each database change sitting in a file. When you're ready to bring your database's schema up to date, just apply any missing migrations, and you're ready to go. There's no need to stress about tracking applied migrations either; Cloudflare will do that for you, and only apply what's needed.

Effectively, any time you want to make a database change, follow these steps:

1. Create a new migration
2. Write the SQL queries to amend the database schemas
3. Apply any missing migrations, including the one you just wrote

For anyone new to the project who needs to get their local development set up, they just have to apply all the migrations, and they're good to go.

Now that you understand how to make changes to a D1 database's schema, go ahead and create your first migration:

```
$ npx wrangler d1 migrations create <DATABASE_NAME> <MIGRATION_NAME>
```

This will create a new folder called migrations, if it doesn't yet exist, in the root directory of your project. You need to replace <DATABASE_NAME> with the name of the database you used when creating the database, and give it a descriptive name for the migration. All the migrations will be stored in that migration folder, in chronological order, so descriptive names help to identify what the migration was seeking to achieve.

For what you are going to be doing in this chapter, run the following command:

```
$ npx wrangler d1 migrations create photo-service initial_creation
```

You'll see the following output; press y when prompted:

```
Ok to create photo-service/migrations? (Y/n)

Successfully created Migration '0000_initial-creation.sql'!

The migration is available for editing here
migrations/0000_initial-creation.sql
```

Now that you have a migration file ready to be filled with SQL, you can write the migration script to make changes to a D1 database.

Create Tables

You can write any SQL you like in a migration file, whether creating tables, adding indexes, inserting data, or even removing data. For now, you'll be creating some tables and inserting some initial data.

Open up the migration file that was created in the migrations folder in the root of your project, and add the SQL shown on the next page:

```
-- Migration number: 0000        2023-04-08T21:27:14.665Z
CREATE TABLE image_categories (
  id INTEGER PRIMARY KEY AUTOINCREMENT,
  slug TEXT UNIQUE,
  display_name TEXT
  created_at TEXT DEFAULT CURRENT_TIMESTAMP
);

INSERT INTO image_categories (slug, display_name) VALUES
('animals', 'Animals'),
('landscapes', 'Landscapes'),
('sports-cars', 'Sports Cars');

CREATE TABLE images (
  id INTEGER PRIMARY KEY AUTOINCREMENT,
  category_id INTEGER NOT NULL,
  user_id INTEGER NOT NULL,
  image_url TEXT NOT NULL,
  title TEXT NOT NULL,
  format TEXT NOT NULL,
  resolution TEXT NOT NULL,
  file_size_bytes INTEGER NOT NULL,
  created_at TEXT DEFAULT CURRENT_TIMESTAMP,
  FOREIGN KEY (category_id) REFERENCES image_categories(id)
);

CREATE INDEX IF NOT EXISTS idx_images_created_at ON images(created_at);

INSERT INTO images
(category_id, user_id, image_url, title,
format, resolution, file_size_bytes)
VALUES
(1, 1, 'https://example.com/some_image.png',
'Example 1', 'PNG', '600x400', 1024),

(2, 2, 'https://example.com/another_image.jpg',
'Example 2', 'JPG', '600x400', 1024),

(2, 3, 'https://example.com/one_more_image.png',
'Example 3', 'PNG', '600x400', 1024),

(3, 4, 'https://example.com/last_mage.jpg',
'Example 4', 'JPG', '600x400', 1024);
```

Make sure you keep the comment at the top of the file. It was created by Cloudflare to keep track of migrations.

There's nothing too fancy going on here: first you create a table to store all the categories that an image can be associated with, and then you seed it with some initial data. Then you create a second table to store the actual images in, with a foreign key between the two tables.

A foreign key ensures referential integrity, so that when an image is inserted with a category, SQLite will validate that the category exists in the image_ categories table before inserting a new row.

Finally, some initial data is seeded into the images table too, so there is some data to work with.

I wanted to keep the number of tables low, so I didn't introduce a linking table to allow an image to be associated with multiple categories, but in most applications that would be a far better choice.

The migration is now written; you can now execute the SQL in the migration against the D1 database that was created.

Run a Migration

You've now created your first migration, which includes creating two tables. You still need to execute that migration though, so the tables are created in the actual D1 database.

To run a migration, you once again use Wrangler. Run the following command from the root of the project:

```
$ npx wrangler d1 migrations apply photo-service --remote
```

Wrangler will first confirm the list of migrations to apply and ask you if you wish to execute them. Press y, and the migrations will be applied to your database in a few seconds. The output will look something like this:

```
Mapping SQL input into an array of statements
Parsing 1 statements
Executing on photo-service (276bd070-ced5-4552-8d4a-07a151764713):
Executed 1 command in 0.04460099991410971ms
Executed 1 command in 0.011500000022351742ms
Mapping SQL input into an array of statements
Parsing 1 statements
Executing on photo-service (276bd070-ced5-4552-8d4a-07a151764713):
Executed 1 command in 9.265480000525711ms
Migrations to be applied:
┌─────────────────────────┐
│ Name                    │
├─────────────────────────┤
│ 0000_create_images.sql  │
└─────────────────────────┘
About to apply 1 migration(s)
Your database may not be available to serve
requests during the migration, continue? … yes
Creating backup...
Mapping SQL input into an array of statements
```

```
Parsing 6 statements
Executing on photo-service (276bd070-ced5-4552-8d4a-07a151764713):
Executed 1 command in 0.5920420000329614ms
Executed 1 command in 2.65099100002350807ms
Executed 1 command in 0.9560579992830752ms
Executed 1 command in 0.913917999714613ms
Executed 1 command in 2.480117999948561ms
Executed 1 command in 26.768490999937057ms
```

Name	Status
0000_create_images.sql	Y

As you can see, Cloudflare takes a backup of your database before applying your migration, and then applies any outstanding migrations. Cloudflare keeps track of the migrations applied so far, so if you were to have three migrations in your repository, and create a brand new database, it would apply all three. If only one migration had been applied, it would apply the other two.

As noted in the output, your database can become unavailable to serve requests when the migration is run. This might be for the backup or due to the SQL you're running. A common case where you may see interruptions is altering tables, such as adding columns. Generally speaking, there should be no downtime, but if you're applying a migration to a large database, consider the approach before running it.

This has only applied the migration to the production database. In a world where you have an application running in production, and you're working on developing the application, you wouldn't want the first migration to be run against production.

Luckily, you can create a local D1 database. All you have to do is replace --remote with --local in the migrations apply command, like so:

```
$ npx wrangler d1 migrations apply photo-service --local
```

The output will mostly look the same, except you'll be prompted initially to create a new local file to store the state of your D1 databases for this project:

```
Mapping SQL input into an array of statements
About to create .wrangler/state/d1/DB.sqlite3, ok? … yes
Loading DB at .wrangler/state/d1/DB.sqlite3
Mapping SQL input into an array of statements
Loading DB at .wrangler/state/d1/DB.sqlite3
```

D1 Backups

An important feature of any database is the ability to create backups. In the event of loss of data or unexpected updates made to the data that you wish to undo, you'll have the ability to retrieve the data that was lost or incorrectly updated. I once managed to accidentally deploy code that updated millions of rows, every single time a form was submitted, rather than just updating the row for the user who submitted the form. I didn't realize it at the time, but I missed the WHERE clause off my query, and this wasn't picked up during testing. Needless to say, I was incredibly thankful the company I worked for had regular backups.

D1 offers some of the best backup functionality I've seen. There is no need to create hourly, daily, or weekly backups because you can restore any D1 database to any point in time in the last thirty days, thanks to a feature Cloudflare calls Time Travel.

You don't need to enable anything, or pay for anything additional; it just comes out of the box with any D1 database. Should you need to restore your database to a former state, you pick when you want to restore it to, and Cloudflare will handle the rest, all via the Cloudflare dashboard or Wrangler.

This is stored per project, so Wrangler will create a new state file each time you run a migration locally for the first time in any project.

With the migration applied to both the production database and local database, the API can now be updated to query the database instead of the in-memory storage!

Retrieve Multiple Rows

While having a database ready to go is great, it's currently not serving an actual function, as it's not being called when the API is accessed.

Cloudflare makes this easy, as it'll inject an object into the Worker at runtime that you can use to query the database. As each endpoint has its own handler in the code you have written, you first need to pass the environment object Cloudflare creates to itty-router so it's available in your handlers.

Open src/index.ts and move the Env interface to a new file at src/env.ts. You'll also need to update the Env interface to add the DB binding:

```
export interface Env {
  DB: D1Database;
}
```

Cloudflare's worker-types package provides a variety of types, with one of them being D1Database, defining the methods available on the object that is injected at runtime.

Next, update the fetch function in src/index.ts:

```
import { Env } from './env';

export default {
  async fetch(
    request: Request,
    env: Env,
    ctx: ExecutionContext
  ): Promise<Response> {
    return router.fetch(request, env);
  },
};
```

The only change here is passing env to the handle method of the router, and including the Env interface that you moved to a separate file. Any binding in the wrangler.toml file will be injected into the env parameter automatically. As a reminder, here's what the binding configuration looks like:

```
[[ d1_databases ]]
binding = "DB" # i.e. available in your Worker on env.DB
database_name = "photo-service"
database_id = "276bd070-ced5-4552-8d4a-07a151764713"
```

This binds a D1 database, whose ID is 276bd070-ced5-4552-8d4a-07a151764713, to the worker. The binding parameter is particularly important, as that's the name you'll use in the code to access the resource, which in this case is the database. As it's called DB, you use env.DB in the code to run queries against the D1 database.

For each resource that's created, whether that's a database or a cache, Cloudflare will provide a simple client API to use. In the case of D1, it provides methods that allow you to prepare SQL queries and execute them against the database.[2]

---

2.   https://developers.cloudflare.com/d1/platform/client-api/

This is much simpler than I'm used to when it comes to the cloud, as there's no need to worry about credentials to access the database, or loading libraries to access the database; Cloudflare does all the heavy lifting for you.

Now that env is being passed to the router, it makes it accessible in the handlers, which is where the application will need to execute any queries.

You can now update the /images endpoint by editing src/handlers/get_images.ts:

```
import { IRequest } from 'itty-router'
import { Env } from '../env';

const getImages = async(request: IRequest, env: Env) => {
  const limit = request.query.count ? request.query.count[0] : 10
  let results;

  try {
    results = await env.DB.prepare(`
      SELECT i.*, c.display_name AS category_display_name
      FROM images i
      INNER JOIN image_categories c ON i.category_id = c.id
      ORDER BY created_at DESC
      LIMIT ?1`
    )
    .bind(limit)
    .all()
  } catch (e) {
    let message;
    if (e instanceof Error) message = e.message;

    console.log({
      message: message
    });

    return new Response('Error', { status: 500 })
  }

  if (!results.success) {
    return new Response(
      'There was a problem retrieving images',
      { status: 500 }
    )
  }

  return new Response(JSON.stringify(results.results), {
    headers: { 'Content-type': 'application/json' }
  });
};

export default getImages;
```

There's quite a lot changed here, so let's step through it.

Firstly, the Env type is imported from env.ts, as you need to provide types for the parameters of the handler. The updated list of parameters can be seen just below that, as the request and env are both passed to the handler.

The next part is where you get to access the database:

```
try {
  results = await env.DB.prepare(`
    SELECT i.*, c.display_name AS category_display_name
    FROM images i
    INNER JOIN image_categories c ON i.category_id = c.id
    ORDER BY created_at DESC
    LIMIT ?1`
  )
  .bind(limit)
  .all()
```

Using env.DB to access the D1 client API, you first prepare an SQL statement. Using prepared statements is good practice, as it helps prevent SQL injection attacks. You shouldn't directly pass values into the prepare method. Instead, you should use ?N, where N is a number. After preparing a statement, you use bind to provide the values that will be used to replace the ?N, with the framework making sure the values are safe.

The number after the question mark represents the order you must bind the parameters. Although you only have one parameter, you can see limit being bound on the next line.

The prepare method will return a statement, which can be used to run a query. There are a number of methods you can use to execute a query against the database. In this case, as you are updating the API endpoint that returns a list of images, you want to call all to return all the results.

The return object will have the following format:

```
{
  results: array | null, // [] if empty, or null if it doesn't apply
  success: boolean, // true if the operation was successful, false otherwise
  meta: {
    duration: number, // duration of the operation in milliseconds
  }
}
```

Therefore, if results were retrieved, you'll see success set to true, and an array of results returned. You can see how long a query took to execute in the meta object, under the duration.

You need to handle the case where the query fails, which happens next:

```
} catch (e) {
  let message;
  if (e instanceof Error) message = e.message;

  console.log({
    message: message
  });

  return new Response('Error', { status: 500 })
}
if (!results.success) {
  return new Response(
    'There was a problem retrieving images',
    { status: 500 }
  )
}
```

The error is logged to the console if an exception is raised, and a 500 HTTP status code returned.

Finally, the response is returned:

```
return new Response(JSON.stringify(results.results), {
  headers: { 'Content-type': 'application/json' }
});
```

As nothing fancy is happening with the response, you can return it as-is from the database. I wouldn't recommend doing this in a real application, as it's coupling the format you store your data in the database to the output in the API. Instead, it's common to have a translation layer between your database and the rest of your code. I've left this out to keep things simple, and focus on what you're here to learn: Cloudflare and serverless.

That's it for retrieving multiple rows from the database, so you can now test it's working as expected by starting the Worker using Wrangler:

```
$ npm run dev
```

If you then hit the GET /images endpoint of your API, which you can do in your browser, you'll see a list of results returned!

When the Worker is started locally, Cloudflare will inject the appropriate binding. As you start the Worker in dev, it injects a binding that will hit the local database you created, with any data stored in the .wrangler folder in your project.

In a lot of cases, you'll perhaps want to retrieve just a single result, so how do you do that?

Prisma ORM

 Over time, Object Relational Mappers (ORM) have become more and more popular. In short, they translate from objects in your codebase to data in your database. For example, you might have a User class that is stored in a users table. When using an ORM, you interact with the User class, and behind the scenes, the ORM handles the translation to and from the database.

If you're more comfortable using an ORM, I recommend checking out https://blog.cloudflare.com/prisma-orm-and-d1 to see how you can use Prisma with Cloudflare.

Retrieve a Single Row

With one API endpoint updated to query D1, you're ready to tackle the endpoint that returns a single image next, before tackling inserting data into the database.

The only changes needed are in the handler that's used when a single image is requested; therefore, you need to edit src/handlers/get_single_image.ts as so:

```
import { IRequest } from 'itty-router'
import { Env } from '../env';

const getSingleImage = async(request: IRequest, env: Env) => {
  let result;

  try {
    result = await env.DB.prepare(`
        SELECT i.*, c.display_name AS category_display_name
        FROM images i
        INNER JOIN image_categories c ON i.category_id = c.id
        WHERE i.id = ?1`
    )
    .bind(request.params.id)
    .first()
  } catch (e) {
    let message;
    if (e instanceof Error) message = e.message;

    console.log({
        message: message
    });

    return new Response('Error', { status: 500 })
  }

  if (!result) {
    return new Response('Not found', { status: 404 })
  }
```

```
  return new Response(JSON.stringify(result), {
    headers: { 'Content-type': 'application/json' }
  });
};
```

```
export default getSingleImage;
```

This is pretty much identical to the get_images.ts handler now, with two minor tweaks. When you were querying the database for multiple rows, you used all. As you are querying for a single result, you can now use first instead:

```
result = await env.DB.prepare(`
    SELECT i.*, c.display_name AS category_display_name
    FROM images i
    INNER JOIN image_categories c ON i.category_id = c.id
    WHERE i.id = ?1`
)
.bind(request.params.id)
.first()
```

This will return the first result from the query, if one is found. If multiple rows are found when the query is executed, you'll only ever see the first one returned. By default, instead of returning a result object, first will return an object representing the first row found.

If you pass the name of a column in the result to first, it'll instead return the value of that column directly. For example:

```
const stmt = db.prepare('SELECT COUNT(1) as img_count FROM images');
const total = await stmt.first('img_count');

// Outputs 5
console.log(total);
```

```
const stmt = db.prepare('SELECT image_url, title FROM images');
const total = await stmt.first();

// outputs {image_url: 'http://www.example.com/foo.png', title: 'Some Title'}
console.log(total);
```

The only other change compared to the API endpoint you've updated already can be seen when the response is returned. As you've just learned, first returns an object representing the row returned, so you simply return that in the response.

If you now run the Worker with npm run dev, you can execute a request against GET /images/:id and see a single result returned.

You're now able to query the D1 database for both GET operations, so let's update the POST to see how you can insert data into a database.

Insert Data

The last endpoint to update is POST /images, which you'll update to insert a row into the database.

Similarly to retrieving data from the database with all and first, you can use the D1 client API to insert data using run. This method returns no results by default, so is perfect for use with INSERT, UPDATE, and DELETE statements.

To update the API to insert records into the database, edit src/handlers/create_image.ts and amend it to the following:

```
import { IRequest } from 'itty-router'
import { Env } from '../env';

const createImage = async(request: IRequest, env: Env) => {
  const json = await request.json()
  let result;

  try {
    result = await env.DB.prepare(`
    INSERT INTO images
    (category_id, user_id, image_url, title,
    format, resolution, file_size_bytes)
    VALUES
    (?1, ?2, ?3, ?4, ?5, ?6, ?7)`
    )
    .bind(
      json.category_id,
      json.user_id,
      json.image_url,
      json.title,
      json.format,
      json.resolution,
      json.file_size_bytes
    )
    .run()
  } catch (e) {
    let message;
    if (e instanceof Error) message = e.message;

    console.log({
      message: message
    });
  }

  if (!result) {
    return new Response('An error occurred', { status: 500 })
  }

  return new Response(
    JSON.stringify(json),
```

```
    {
      status: 201,
      headers: { 'Content-type': 'application/json' }
    }
  );
}

export default createImage;
```

Once again, this should look very familiar, as it's almost identical to the prior two handlers. The main difference is with the query, so let's take a closer look at that:

```
try {
  result = await env.DB.prepare(`
    INSERT INTO images
    (category_id, user_id, image_url, title,
    format, resolution, file_size_bytes)
    VALUES
    (?1, ?2, ?3, ?4, ?5, ?6, ?7)`
  )
  .bind(
    json.category_id,
    json.user_id,
    json.image_url,
    json.title,
    json.format,
    json.resolution,
    json.file_size_bytes
  )
  .run()
```

Yet again, you're using prepare. This time, you have a lot of placeholder values to insert, identified with the ?N in the VALUES part of the query. You can see the numbers at play here more than before, as json.category_id is mapped to ?1, json.user_id mapped to ?2 and so forth.

As I just mentioned, run returns no results, so the input to the API is used in the response to the client.

However, you have an ID column that is auto-generated when a row is inserted, and that is currently missing from the response. If you do want to insert data and retrieve the response, for use in the output, you need to update the query, as shown on the next page:

```
result = await env.DB.prepare(`
  INSERT INTO images
  (category_id, user_id, image_url, title, format, resolution, file_size_bytes)
  VALUES
  (?1, ?2, ?3, ?4, ?5, ?6, ?7)
  RETURNING *;`
)
.bind(
  json.category_id,
  json.user_id,
  json.image_url,
  json.title,
  json.format,
  json.resolution,
  json.file_size_bytes
)
.first()
```

In this query, RETURNING *; has been added and first used instead of run. In SQLite, RETURNING will return any rows that were inserted, updated, or deleted by the query. This is a handy way to avoid executing a SELECT query after an insert, as you can effectively do them both in a single query.

To see the response containing the ID from the database, simply update the response that is returned like so:

```
return new Response(
    JSON.stringify(result),
    {
      status: 201,
      headers: { 'Content-type': 'application/json' }
    }
);
```

That's all the changes needed, so once again, you can start the Worker with npm run dev and issue a request to POST /images. You can then check it was inserted by issuing a GET /images request afterward.

From your terminal, first issue a POST request to create an image:

```
$ curl --location 'http://0.0.0.0:8787/images' \
  --header 'Content-Type: application/json'     \
  --data '{ "category_id": 2,
            "user_id": 100,
            "image_url": "https://placehold.co/600x400",
            "format": "PNG",
            "resolution": "100x100",
            "title": "Example 4",
            "file_size_bytes": 500 }'
```

Make sure that you check the port number is the same as the port output when you run npm run dev. A new image should be inserted, and you can check it has been by trying to retrieve it using its ID, replacing your-id-goes-here with the id returned in the POST response:

```
$ curl --location 'http://0.0.0.0:8787/images/your-id-goes-here'
```

That's it for databases. Congratulations on building your first API with Cloudflare and serverless!

Connecting to Third-Party Databases

 If you already have a significant amount of data stored in a database, you may want to move your compute to Cloudflare Workers but keep your existing database. This is supported by Cloudflare, allowing you to connect from Workers to a variety of databases, including Postgres, Supabase, Prisma, MongoDB and many more.

How to connect your Worker to an external database varies per database and provider, with each database and provider being documented in Cloudflare's documentation.[3]

A promising new addition to Cloudflare is Hyperdrive, which accelerates queries from your Workers to externally-hosted databases, including intelligently caching data.

What You've Learned

In this chapter, you learned the core concepts of using a serverless database, such as Cloudflare D1. You learned how to connect that database to a Worker using the wrangler.toml file, using bindings. You explored migrations, which you used to create your first set of tables in D1. And you updated your API to make use of the newly created database, learning how to read and write data to the database.

There is one more feature to go over before you move on from APIs: implementing Worker-to-Worker calls.

---

3. https://developers.cloudflare.com/workers/databases/connecting-to-databases/

## CHAPTER 5

Worker-to-Worker Communication

Your API is almost complete, but there's one thing we haven't covered yet: Worker-to-Worker communication.

In typical software architectures, when you're not dealing with a monolith, you'll likely need your services to talk to each other through API calls. With serverless architectures, it's not smart to squeeze everything into one Worker, so truly monolithic apps are pretty rare.

If you've got multiple APIs contributing to your app, I'd suggest using multiple Workers. Traditionally, these calls between services happen over HTTP, and whether they're private or public, they have to deal with network-related issues like latency and failures.

But here's the cool part with Cloudflare: Worker-to-Worker communication is a breeze. Just like how you added a database as a dependency to the Photo API using a binding, you can do the same with other Workers. They're called service bindings.

When Cloudflare fires up a Worker with a service binding, it makes the second Worker instantly available to the primary Worker. No latency, no delays, and no worries about networking hiccups like you'd have with HTTP calls. In software engineering, this is often called a zero-cost abstraction. In short, this means it gives you benefits without any drawbacks.

Service bindings not only make your apps more reliable and less prone to failures, compared to traditional HTTP calls, but they also promote composability and fine-grained Workers without any extra performance cost when communicating between them. It really is a beautiful feature.

When one Worker sends a request over to another, the cost is straightforward—you just get billed for the CPU time that Worker uses; it doesn't add to your overall request count. This effectively makes service bindings free.

Now, to get the hang of making API calls between different Workers, you're going to make one last change to your Photo API. You'll add a second Worker to bring some authentication into the mix. When you're dealing with multiple APIs scattered across different Workers, this move makes it super easy to apply consistent authentication across the board.

You're effectively creating a new Worker that behaves like middleware.

To understand how Worker-to-Worker calls function, let's see them in action.

Create the Authentication Worker

You'll use the same steps as in Chapter 1, Deploy Your First Cloudflare Worker, on page 1, to create the authentication Worker:

```
$ npm create cloudflare@2.21.1 -- --no-auto-update
```

I suggest running this one level above your photo-service Worker, so the folder structure would look like this:

```
photo-service/
├── .wrangler/
├── migrations/
├── node_nodules/
├── src/
├── test/
authentication-service/
├── node_nodules/
├── src/
```

When running the command, enter authentication-service for the directory, select "Hello World" for the Worker type, yes to TypeScript, and yes to Git.

With the skeleton of the authentication Worker created, you can now add the specific changes needed for the authentication Worker.

Make a Worker Private

In the case of the photo service, that API would be public facing. So when you deploy to Cloudflare, you get a URL generated that allows you to hit it with requests.

Sometimes, you might not want your service to be accessible to the outside world. Take the authentication service, for example—no need for it to be out there publicly since it's always called by a service binding.

Monorepo vs. Many Repos

There are two common approaches for arranging the pieces that make up an application. The first is the approach we just used: two separate folders, each with its own repositor0y under version control. You'd make changes to each project individually, and each would be deployed separately.

The alternative approach is called a *monorepo:* all the services are stored together in a single repository. When you merge changes to the monorepo, any services updated will all be deployed. You may still need to deploy services in a certain order, which can be handled by your deployment pipeline, but the trigger will be a single merge to the monorepo.

Monorepos can be slower to deploy, but you can mitigate a lot of this by only deploying the individual services that were changed. There's a risk of compolexity: if you don't keep it organized, it can become unwieldy and complicated, with dependencies often hard to work out and manage.

Which one is right for your project is going to come down to the individual project. I'd recommend trying out both approaches, and seeing which one works for you.

A monorepo is great for sharing code between projects, so an alternative to my approach in this chapter would have authentication logic as a library shared between your many APIs.

Making a Worker private is achieved by disabling the auto-generated URL, which is a simple configuration change. Open wrangler.toml in your authentication Worker, and add the following line to the bottom:

```
workers_dev = false
```

That's all there is to it. If you now deploy this Worker, you'd see no URL was generated based on your account's subdomain, effectively making it private and unreachable via the public internet.

When deploying to production, you'll most likely want a custom domain associated with the photo service. We cover that in Chapter 15, Deploy to Production, on page 213. To keep the authentication Worker private, you simply wouldn't assign a custom domain.

With the Worker now private, let's add the authentication logic.

Add Authentication Logic

The last change you need to make to the authentication service is to actually add some authentication logic. Now, just a heads-up; you're keeping it dead simple for this demo, but in the real world, I'd advise a more robust approach like OAuth with JWT tokens for authentication.

We'll use a shared secret key to authenticate requests. Whoever's calling the API puts that secret key into the header of the HTTP request. The authentication service will then cross-check that header value with the secret key.

Let's add the code to the Worker, inside of src/index.ts:

```
export interface Env {
  API_AUTH_KEY: String;
}

export default {
        async fetch(
    request: Request,
    env: Env,
    ctx: ExecutionContext
  ): Promise<Response> {
    const api_key = request.headers.get('x-api-auth-key');

    if (api_key === env.API_AUTH_KEY) {
      return new Response('Authenticated', { status: 200 });
    }

    return new Response('Unauthorized', { status: 401 });
  }
};
```

As you can see, the logic is straightforward. The Worker retrieves the x-api-auth-key header, and compares it with the secret that's stored in env.API_AUTH_KEY. If it's a match, the Worker returns a 200, if it's not, it returns a 401.

You'll perhaps notice API_AUTH_KEY defined in the Env interface at the top. But how does that value get set?

Store Application Secrets

In many apps, you've got to store some confidential stuff—like a password for an API—and you definitely don't want that just hanging around in plain sight or ending up in version control.

If you're familiar with AWS, you might've tackled this with AWS Secrets Manager. It's a bit of a chore, creating secrets, tying them to keys in KMS, and wrestling with IAM policies. Cloudflare makes it a breeze, and it's still totally secure.

Like bindings (e.g. databases), secrets can be injected into your Worker through the env parameter. You've already coded your Worker to expect API_AUTH_KEY, so you'll add in a secret with the same name. Cloudflare handles the injection at runtime for you automatically.

As a bonus, you can switch up the secret for each environment. You know how it goes in most companies—production, staging, and maybe a few other environments. When you create secrets, tag them with an environment flag, and Cloudflare will serve up the right secret for that environment when your Worker runs.

For now, you will just create one global secret, as environments will be covered in greater detail in Chapter 15, Deploy to Production, on page 213. Creating a new secret in Cloudflare is a one-liner; make sure you run it in the authentication service folder:

```
$ wrangler secret put API_AUTH_KEY
```

Once you execute that line, you'll be prompted to enter the secret's value. It will be obfuscated so it's not visible in your terminal's logs, and you can enter any alphanumeric characters you like, plus symbols. I chose mysupersecretkey, but feel free to use whatever secret you like.

As a secret is stored against a Worker in production; if you run this command without first deploying your Worker, Cloudflare will create an empty project to store the secret in. You can see this by going to the dashboard after storing the secret. If the Worker is already deployed, it simply adds the secret under Settings > Variables.

Cloudflare will encrypt and store your secret against a given Worker, so once you've stored a secret, it's impossible to view its value.

When deployed, this secret will be injected into the authentication Worker when a request is executed against it. This means locally, you need to add an extra file to set any secrets you need when developing a Worker.

To do this, add a new file in the root directory of the authentication service named .dev.vars and add the following to it:

```
API_AUTH_KEY=mysupersecretkey
```

If you've ever used env files before, it's effectively the same pattern. Using env files is a common pattern to set local environment variables that are needed to run an application locally. You add any environment variables you need in the file and make sure that file is not committed to version control by adding it to the list of ignored files. When the application is started, you can load the values from the env file, or in a lot of cases, such as this one, the framework will handle that for you and automatically load them.

If you want to set environment variables that are not secret, you can add them to .dev.vars too for local development. To ensure they are set when you deploy to Cloudflare, you can use vars in your wrangler.toml file:

```
[vars]
API_HOST = "example.com"
```

This would then be available under env.API_HOST. This isn't necessary for this project, so no need to add any vars to your wrangler.toml file.

That's all the changes you need to make to the authentication Worker, so let's check it works as you expected.

Test the Authentication Worker

Although you disabled URLs for this Worker, you still get a URL locally when you run a Worker with npm run dev. You won't be directly calling this Worker in the application, but you can still test its functionality is working as expected, as it's still just a Worker at the end of the day.

Each time you start a Worker, make sure you note the port that it has been started on. Cloudflare will typically start your Worker on port 8787, but if that one isn't available, it'll pick another one that is.

The authentication Worker picks up the secret value from .dev.vars:

```
Using vars defined in .dev.vars
Your worker has access to the following bindings:
- Vars:
  - API_AUTH_KEY: "(hidden)"
⎔ Listening at http://0.0.0.0:8787
- http://127.0.0.1:8787
- http://192.168.1.90:8787
```

To test it's applying the authentication logic, you can hit it with some requests. First, let's not pass any headers:

```
$ curl http://0.0.0.0:8787
Unauthorized
```

As you would expect, the Worker returns an unauthorized response. If you look in the terminal window where your authentication Worker is running,

```
$ curl http://0.0.0.0:8787 -H "x-api-auth-key:wrong"
Unauthorized
```

Once again, as you'd expect, an unauthorized response is returned. Now let's try with the correct secret:

```
$ curl http://0.0.0.0:8787 -H "x-api-auth-key:mysupersecretkey"
Authenticated
```

When you provide the correct secret, the Worker indicates that the request was authenticated, so everything is working as expected. Therefore, the authentication Worker is ready to be used to authenticate requests to the photo API, which we'll implement next.

Add a Service Binding

You now need to use the authentication Worker, and start authenticating requests to the photo API. To enable calls between Workers that do not go via the public internet, you need to use a service binding.

To add a service binding to a Worker, you once again make a change in the wrangler.toml. Open that file in the photo API, and add the following line:

```
services = [
  { binding = "AUTH", service = "authentication-service" }
]
```

Place this snippet above the D1 database definition for proper TOML formatting. In TOML, all key-value pairs must come before any tables. Since you set up the D1 database using a table, your service binding should be positioned above that table. You can go with either format to add resources to your Workers—I've used a mix to show both options.

As you can see, services is an array, so you can bind multiple Workers.

Now, on to the binding details. Two keys to pay attention to: first, the binding's name for your code, and second, the Worker's name configured with service. Make sure the service key aligns with the name in the wrangler.toml for the Worker you want to bind.

If you now start the photo service Worker using npm run dev, you'll notice it lists the binding during startup. (The output is on the next page.)

```
Your worker has access to the following bindings:
- D1 Databases:
  - DB: photo-service (XXX)
- Services:
  - AUTH: authentication-service
⎵ Listening at http://0.0.0.0:8787
- http://127.0.0.1:8787
- http://192.168.1.90:8787
```

You have two options to test a service binding. You can either publish any Workers that are bound to the Worker you're running locally; in your case, the authentication Worker. Alternatively, you can run everything strictly locally, and Wrangler will keep track of locally-running Workers and route them accordingly on your device.

For the first method, you need to run npm run deploy in the root of your authentication Worker, and then start the photo service using npm run dev. This has the downside of your local testing hitting the production version of the authentication service.

The second method will be covered below.

Before you try calling the Workers though, you first need to add the logic in the photo service to authenticate requests. Firstly, introduce the service binding into the environment interface in src/env.ts:

```
export interface Env {
  DB: D1Database;
  AUTH: Fetcher;
}
```

The key must match the name you defined in the wrangler.toml file, and the type is Fetcher, which is a simple interface to the Fetch API. Communication between Workers is handled using fetch, and although the interface looks like it's HTTP, the underlying networking is not. As mentioned, Worker-to-Worker communication does not go via HTTP, and uses internal Cloudflare magic to route requests.

With the service binding added to the environment, Cloudflare will inject the necessary dependency at runtime. In this case, it will give your photo service Worker access to the authentication Worker.

Update the fetch method in src/index.ts in your photo service Worker like so:

```
export default {
  async fetch(
    request: Request,
    env: Env,
    ctx: ExecutionContext
  ): Promise<Response> {
    const auth_response = await env.AUTH.fetch(request.clone());

    if (auth_response.status !== 200) {
      return auth_response;
    }

    return router.fetch(request, env);
  },
};
```

There isn't too much change here: you've simply added a few lines before trying to route the request to the right handler. The first line calls the authentication Worker, passing a copy of the request. You have to clone it as a request object can only be read once per HTTP call to a Worker. Once you call a method such as request.json(), doing so again will result in an error.

With this setup, you're making a copy of the incoming request when you call the authentication Worker. If you need to, you could tweak the request before passing it in, or even create a brand new one. Think of it like using a service binding as middleware. In the real world, you might have to call a whole separate API with a totally different request, like so:

```
await env.PAYMENT_SERVICE.fetch('http://example.com/payments');
```

In this case, a GET request is being made to a fictitious payment service, and not simply passing the request through. Similarly, for POST requests, you can create a new request object and call fetch with that. One thing to note is you must provide an absolute URL when calling between Workers using service bindings. Even though the request is not sent via HTTP, you must provide a hostname. It doesn't matter what that hostname is though; you can literally use anything.

Lastly, the response from the authentication Worker is checked to ensure only authenticated requests are handled by your photo API. If the authentication Worker responds that the request is not authenticated, the response from the authentication Worker is returned.

That's all the code changes needed, so you can now see the service binding in action.

Test a Service Binding

At present, calling between two Workers locally is an experimental feature. The feature is being actively worked on, so feel free to give it a try, but if it doesn't work you'll need to run both on Cloudflare's servers.

First, deploy the authentication service using npm run deploy in the authentication-service folder. Once deployed, you can run the photo service from your device, but you must run it remotely on Cloudflare's servers. Therefore, start the photo service with npm run dev -- --remote in the photo-service folder.

One thing to note is that this will mean requests will hit the production version of your Worker.

With the authentication service deployed and the photo service running remotely from your device, you can hit the photo service with a simple GET request initially not passing the API key:

```
$ curl http://127.0.0.1:8787/images/
Unauthorized
```

As you didn't pass an API key, this is exactly what you expected. If you now pass the API key, you should see a list of photos being returned as JSON:

```
$ curl "http://127.0.0.1:8787/images/?count=1" \
-H "x-api-auth-key:mysupersecretkey"
[
  {
    "id": 1,
    "category_id": 1,
    "user_id": 1,
    "image_url": "https://example.com/some_image.png",
    "title": "Example 1",
    "format": "PNG",
    "resolution": "600x400",
    "file_size_bytes": 1024,
    "created_at": "2023-07-22 22:06:23",
    "category_display_name": "Animals"
  }
]
```

I trimmed the full response down to one result, just to make the output easier to see, but it worked—the photo service is now calling the authentication Worker on each request to ensure the correct authentication is provided.

What You've Learned

In this chapter, you've taken a deep dive into service bindings and how you can enable Worker-to-Worker communication.

This is the last chapter you'll be working on this API, as you've now seen the essentials of Workers. Using these techniques, you'll be able to deploy any back end you want. Both the photo service and authentication Worker code are available to view on GitHub.[1,2]

However, a lot of applications don't simply have a back end, they also have a front end.

In the next chapter, you'll learn how to deploy front end applications to Cloudflare.

---

1. https://github.com/apeacock1991/serverless-apps-on-cloudflare/tree/main/photo-service
2. https://github.com/apeacock1991/serverless-apps-on-cloudflare/tree/main/authentication-service

## CHAPTER 6

Build a Static Website with Pages

So far, you've been working exclusively with APIs, but for most websites and projects, you need some kind of static content. Whether it's a blog, a simple content site, or a landing page, having something that delivers static content is essential.

There are many choices for hosting static content. You can opt for shared hosting with a monthly fee, use a platform like Squarespace, or take a more technical route with AWS S3 and a linked domain. The possibilities for deploying static content online are endless.

When a company I worked for needed to host a new static application, I explored what Cloudflare had to offer. Cloudflare Pages, designed to provide the basics for building websites, was the answer I was looking for.

Shared hosting requires manual setup and FTP uploads. Squarespace handles everything, but lacks version control and full customization. AWS S3, while an option, shares deployment and file management challenges with shared hosting.

Both S3 and shared hosting serve content from one region, causing potential latency for worldwide users. AWS S3 somewhat addresses this with Cloud-Front, but it introduces complexity and extra costs. You'd think, given the web's origin in static HTML pages, deploying them would still be quick and straightforward.

Cloudflare Pages does exactly that: a simple and straightforward product to deploy static content with ease.

Just like with Workers, you focus on your code and Cloudflare serves it to your users. Pages is versatile, supporting most popular JS frameworks, including Next.js, React, Vite, Astro, Svelte, as well as simpler ones like Hugo or Jekyll. As of now, it covers over twenty-five frameworks, and essentially, any framework generating a static website at build time is compatible, or even a site built using your own custom framework.

In the upcoming chapter, I'll guide you through building a fully static website using Next.js and deploying it on Cloudflare.

You'll build a straightforward weather application that lets users check the weather in different cities worldwide. For now, you're focusing on the front end, so no dynamic features, no actual weather forecasts, and the app's data will be hard-coded.

Cloudflare Pages also supports full-stack websites too, so in Chapter 7, Add a Back End to the Front End, on page 79, you'll learn how to add a back end to the weather application, and later you'll learn how to cache data for improved performance in Chapter 8, Cache Data with KV, on page 97.

Here's a visual preview of what you'll be creating. Circled numbers show the new elements introduced in each chapter. The numbers in the diamonds depict the sequence of interactions when the application processes a request.

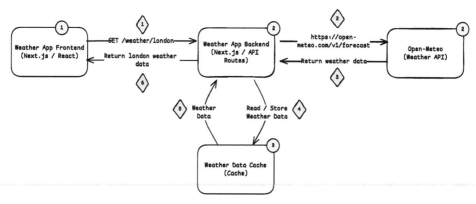

In this chapter, you'll learn how to bootstrap a new Pages project, add some content to it, and deploy it to Cloudflare Pages.

Create a Pages Project

To get started, you need to create a new Pages project. You do this in the same way you created a Worker, using npm create. Any time you want to create a new project, whether it's a Worker or Pages project, I would always reach for this option.

First, execute the following command:

```
$ npm create cloudflare@2.21.1 -- --no-auto-update
```

Static Assets Workers

At the time of writing, a new type of Worker is currently in beta. This new type of Worker is called a Static Assets Worker, and it specializes in serving static assets directly from files within your codebase.

As Cloudflare Workers cannot read from the file system, serving static assets from Workers has traditionally been tricky—you had to upload them to R2, or use Pages, which drastically simplified the approach of serving static websites.

In the future, I suspect that Static Assets Workers will become the de facto way to deploy websites as well as APIs, so I think it's important to cover those too. You'll build an application using them in Chapter 13, WebSockets with Durable Objects, on page 171.

The first prompt will ask for the name you want to use for the project. I chose to use weather-app.

For the second prompt, you select Website or web app, followed by Next, as you'll be using Next.js for this application.

I chose Next.js because it's the framework I'm most familiar with, and its straightforward project structure makes it ideal for illustrating how to build on Cloudflare. Additionally, integrating a back end will be a breeze, mirroring the process on any other Next.js application hosted elsewhere.

You'll learn about the specifics later, but essentially, when Cloudflare builds the project, it adapts certain elements to function on their platform. Fortunately, this requires no special handling; the build process takes care of it seamlessly, allowing you to build a Next.js app just as you normally would.

Once you've selected Next.js, select the following options as they are asked:

- Use TypeScript
- Don't use ESLint
- Don't use Tailwind CSS
- Use the src folder
- Use the app router
- Don't customize the default import aliases
- Don't deploy your application

The project will now be created using the configuration you selected.

By default, Next.js operates with the full Node runtime, designed for continuous processes on traditional cloud platforms like AWS EC2. However, Cloudflare, being serverless, doesn't support continuous processes. Instead, Cloudflare manages requests without maintaining continuous processes for serverless functions. It spins up small isolates to handle incoming requests, eliminating the need to run a process 24/7.

Behind the scenes, Cloudflare Pages uses the same mechanism as Workers to serve content. Essentially, bespoke internal Workers, specifically tailored for full-stack applications, power Cloudflare Pages, providing a streamlined interface for engineers.

As you know, Cloudflare operates on the edge and currently doesn't fully support Node. When running a Next.js application on Cloudflare, it operates in edge mode, aligning with Cloudflare's runtime. Although Next.js offers a serverless runtime option, positioned between the edge and Node runtimes, it's not suitable for Cloudflare at this time due to its dependency on the full Node runtime.

According to Next.js documentation, the edge runtime provides a significant speed advantage. Even the serverless runtime, with an average start time of 250ms, can't match the 0ms delay on Cloudflare's edge runtime. Given the emphasis on speed and performance by search engines, this difference can impact your website's ranking.

During the bootstrapping of your application, you may have noticed a special Cloudflare adapter being added to your project:

Adding the Cloudflare Pages adapter

Cloudflare provides its own adapter for Next.js, and several other frameworks, which is used at build time to prepare your application for deployment on their platform. If you're accustomed to using Next.js, you won't detect any differences in the actual application code at this stage, as this adapter operates solely during the build process for now. When you build your application, Cloudflare organizes the output to align with their platform.

With that, your Next.js project has been created and is ready to run on Cloudflare, requiring minimal effort. Next, let's dive into the basic structure that Next.js has set up, in case you're not already familiar with it.

Understand the Project Structure

If you've used Next.js before, you can probably skip this section, as it'll just be reviewing the default structure that's created by Next.js. With the introduction of version 13 of Next.js, the default paradigm for projects uses the new app router, replacing the pages router that existed before it. Both are still currently supported, but this project will exclusively use the app router as that's the future direction of Next.js.

You don't need to look at every single folder and file created, but you should look at the main ones. Here's a rough outline of the project structure as it currently stands:

```
weather-app/
├─ public/
├─ src/
│   ├─ app/
│   │   ├─ api/
│   │   │   ├─ hello/
│   │   │   │   ├─ route.ts
│   │   │   ├─ hello.ts
│   │   ├─ globals.css
│   │   ├─ layout.tsx
│   │   ├─ page.module.css
│   │   ├─ page.tsx
├─ next.config.js
├─ package.json
├─ package-lock.json
└─ wrangler.toml
```

It's pretty lightweight, as there isn't really any content in the bootstrapped project that has been created for us.

In the root folder, you have a few files you're likely already familiar with, starting with wrangler.toml. As a reminder, this is where you define the dependencies of your Worker in the form of bindings. This file works in exactly the same way as it does for a Worker, used both during local development and deployment.

Next up, there are package.json and package-lock.json, which are used by npm to maintain the packages used by an application. Most packages listed there are as you'd expect— next, react, and so forth. However, under devDependencies, you'll see two that are specifically needed for Cloudflare:

```
"devDependencies": {
    "@cloudflare/next-on-pages": "^1.5.0",
    "vercel": "^30.2.3"
}
```

I've briefly mentioned the @cloudflare/next-on-pages package; it's currently used to ready your application for Cloudflare during the build. In Chapter 8, Cache Data with KV, on page 97, you'll make use of the adapter to access the bindings for your Pages project.

The second package is the Vercel CLI, which Cloudflare uses for deploying your application. It's worth noting that Vercel is another serverless hosting provider, similar to Cloudflare, and it's run by the creators of Next.js. While you don't need to comprehend its inner workings, you'll observe in the build logs during build time that these two packages are being used.

Now, let's explore the src folder, where you'll add and update the code. Inside src, there's the app directory, adopting the app router structure for the project. Many frameworks use this structure, so you've likely encountered it before.

In essence, each folder within the app folder corresponds to a route, mapping to the URL structure of your application. With the current folder structure, there's src/app/api/hello/route.ts. When the application runs, this sets up an API endpoint at /api/hello, with the endpoint's logic residing in route.ts.

In this example is a server-side endpoint, so it uses a route.ts file. If you wanted to render a UI page instead, you would add a page.tsx file instead of a route.ts file.

I don't want to get too in-depth on the workings of Next.js, as that's not the focus of this book, but it's important you understand some fundamentals to follow along. You can read more about the app router in Next.js here.[1]

Finally, you have a few more files in src/app. For now, you only need a couple of them, but it's worth going over them briefly. There are two .css files, global.css and page.module.css. The global.css file contains any CSS that is used across your application, so things like headers and footers that are identical across pages. A page.module.css can be included alongside any page.tsx to include page-specific CSS for that page. This helps scope CSS to specific pages, reducing bloat in your CSS, as only the CSS needed for that page is returned to the browser.

The last two files are page.tsx and layout.tsx. In layout.tsx you'll see the following:

```
import './globals.css'
import { Inter } from 'next/font/google'

const inter = Inter({ subsets: ['latin'] })
```

---

1. https://nextjs.org/docs/app/building-your-application/routing#the-app-router

```
export const metadata = {
  title: 'Create Next App',
  description: 'Generated by create next app',
}

export default function RootLayout({
  children,
}: {
  children: React.ReactNode
}) {
  return (
    <html lang="en">
      <body className={inter.className}>{children}</body>
    </html>
  )
}
```

Effectively, this is the global layout for the application. The content for each page is then injected into {children}, allowing you to have the same layout, such as headers and footers, across different pages. You can adjust the layout across different routes too, if you wish. For example, you could create src/app/docs/ and include a layout.tsx file, and the layout defined there would be used for any pages in the docs folder, rather than the layout defined in the root of the app folder.

The second file is the page.tsx file, which contains the page-specific content. It looks something like this:

```
import styles from './page.module.css'

export default function Home() {
// Page-specific markup goes here
}
```

I've omitted the content for brevity, but anything in the Home function will be used as the content for this page. As it's in the root of the app folder, this page.tsx will be used to render the home page of your application. For other pages, the function name would be Page instead of Home.

You don't need quite a few of these files for now, so let's remove some of them:

```
$ rm -rf src/app/api src/app/globals.css src/app/page.module.css
```

This will remove the hello API, and some of the CSS files that you won't need. This will help to keep the project clean, as you'll add your own API in the next chapter.

That covers the default project structure for a fresh Next.js application. Now that you understand how the project is structured, let's start building the static version of the application.

Install Bootstrap

With the base project set up, you can start adding the specific things you'll need for the weather application. To keep things simple style-wise, you're going to use Bootstrap. For those not familiar, it's a simple front end framework that contains all the core CSS any website would need, such as columns, rows, and menus.

To save you from having to download and reference Bootstrap, you use the npm package. You can add it to any project using the following command:

```
npm install bootstrap prop-types --save
```

This will install the npm package for you locally, and add it to the package.json file. You're also adding prop-types, which allows you to validate data is correctly passed in React components—you'll use this later on.

With Bootstrap installed and ready to go, you can add the layout and home page to the project.

Create the Home Page

The first thing you're going to build is the home page of the application. It'll be incredibly simple, with just a heading, a select field with a few locations in it, a button to find the weather for the selected location, and finally, a little box to show the weather in that location.

For now, all of the elements will be visible on the page. Once you add dynamic functionality with a back end, the weather information will be hidden initially, until a location is selected.

To give you an idea of what you're building, here's what the end result will look like:

Check the weather forecast

London, UK   Check!

New York, US
Current temperature: 5.42°C
Windspeed: 12kph

To achieve this, you'll need to edit two files you've already looked at. The first one is in src/app/layout.tsx, and you'll need to update it to the following:

```
import 'bootstrap/dist/css/bootstrap.css';
import { Inter } from 'next/font/google'

const inter = Inter({ subsets: ['latin'] })

export const metadata = {
  title: 'Weather App',
  description: 'See the weather, anywhere in the world (sort of)',
}

export default function RootLayout({
  children,
}: {
  children: React.ReactNode
}) {
  return (
    <html lang="en">
      <body className={inter.className}>
        {children}
      </body>
    </html>
  )
}
```

For the most part, this isn't too different from the default layout.tsx that ships with Next.js. There are a few changes though:

1. Bootstrap CSS is included by importing it, and you removed the import for the globals.css file.

2. The metadata was updated to reflect what the application does.

The larger changes come in the actual page content. To update that, you need to amend src/app/page.tsx:

```
export default function Home() {
  return (
    <section className="vh-100">
      <div className="container py-5 h-100">

        <div className="row d-flex justify-content-center align-items-center
            h-100">
          <div className="col-md-8 col-lg-6 col-xl-4">

            <h3 className="mb-4 pb-2 fw-normal">
              Check the weather forecast now
            </h3>

            <div className="input-group rounded mb-3">
            <select className="form-control rounded" aria-label="Search"
                aria-describedby="search-addon" id="location-select">
```

```
              <option value="london">London, UK</option>
              <option value="new-york">New York, US</option>
              <option value="los-angeles">Los Angeles, US</option>
              <option value="berlin">Berlin, Germany</option>
              <option value="tokyo">Tokyo, Japan</option>
            </select>
            <a href="#"
               type="button"
               style={{textDecoration: 'none'}}>

              <span className="input-group-text border-0 fw-bold"
                    id="search-addon"
                    style={{background: 'none'}}>
              Check!
              </span>
            </a>
          </div>

          <div className="card shadow-0 border">
            <div className="card-body p-4">
              <h4 className="mb-1 sfw-normal">
                New York, US
              </h4>
              <p className="mb-2">
                Current temperature: <strong>5.42°C</strong>
              </p>
              <p className="mb-2">
                Windspeed: <strong>12kph</strong>
              </p>
            </div>
          </div>

        </div>
      </div>

    </div>
  </section>
  )
}
```

This part is quite straightforward, but let's quickly walk through it. As you edit the page.tsx file at the root of the app folder, this page gets rendered when someone visits the home page. All you're doing here is returning the markup for that page.

Although it might resemble HTML, it's JSX from the React framework. If you haven't worked with React before, no worries — I'll guide you through everything, and grasping the basics is remarkably straightforward.

That covers the layout and content needed for the static version of the application. Before deploying, let's make sure it looks as expected when accessed locally.

Run the Static Website Locally

With the static website complete, you can take a look at the weather application in all its glory locally, ensuring it looks as expected before deploying to Cloudflare.

There are several ways to run it locally, and I usually opt for a practical approach based on the situation. At this point, since the application isn't leveraging any Cloudflare features, you can simply use npm run dev to launch Next.js locally.

Visit http://localhost:3000 to preview the website. This method is the quickest and easiest for static applications. Just be mindful of any other processes using port 3000; if needed, check the port specified when running npm run dev, as Next.js will choose an alternative if 3000 is in use.

Before deploying, it's wise to confirm everything functions as expected in Cloudflare's actual runtime.

It's a two-step process, as you need to build the application first, and then run it locally—but this time, in Cloudflare's workerd runtime. As part of the creation of the project, Cloudflare created a handy npm script to do this all for you:

```
npm run preview
```

When you run this command, the Next.js-specific Cloudflare adapter is used to build the application in such a way that it's compatible with Cloudflare. Then, the output from the build is, by default, stored in .vercel/output/. The second part of the preview command runs wrangler pages dev .vercel/output/static, which will retrieve the built application from .vercel/output/ and run it locally in Cloudflare's runtime. This is all nicely wrapped up for you by npm run preview.

The same process happens when you deploy to production, except it's deployed to Cloudflare's production environment, rather being spun up locally.

Once you've run the command, you can typically access your Pages application at http://127.0.0.1:8787/. The port may vary, so make sure you check the output in your terminal. When accessing that URL, your application is being served from Cloudflare's network.

While it's useful to be able to preview your application in Cloudflare's runtime, I opt for `npm run dev` most of the time because it's significantly faster than deploying to Cloudflare's runtime. This speed difference stems from the fact that every time a change is made, the application needs to be rebuilt, a process that takes at least a few seconds.

When using `npm run dev`, you get advantages like code reloading without restarting the application. Additionally, since it's a purely static website at this stage, testing on Cloudflare doesn't offer any real advantage. Essentially, it's just a vanilla Next.js application for now.

When you look at adding dynamic functionality in Chapter 7, Add a Back End to the Front End, on page 79, and integrating a Cloudflare service with the application, you'll look at ways you can fine-tune your local development.

With the application working locally, the final step is to deploy the application.

Deploy a Pages Application

As you've come to expect from Cloudflare, deploying an application to Cloudflare Pages is a breeze, and can be done from the comfort of your terminal. Similarly to building and running your application locally, Cloudflare has added a script to deploy your application too:

```
$ npm run deploy
```

This script will build your application first, then deploy it to Cloudflare. You'll be asked to create a new project in your Cloudflare account when you deploy, so go ahead and let it create one.

Once complete, you'll see the URL where your application is available printed in the terminal:

```
Uploading... (30/30)

Success! Uploaded 5 files (25 already uploaded) (1.53 sec)

Uploading _headers
Compiled Worker successfully
Uploading Worker bundle
Uploading _routes.json
Deployment complete!

Take a peek over at https://some-hash.xxx-app-5hu.pages.dev
```

When you visit that URL, you'll see the static version of the weather app. In Chapter 15, Deploy to Production, on page 213, you'll learn how to integrate custom domains into projects, rather than using the auto-generated ones Cloudflare provides.

Cloudflare offers two deployment environments for Pages: preview and production. The environment you deploy to is determined by the branch's name that you're working on. The initial branch pushed to production becomes the production branch, while any subsequent branches are treated as preview branches. This setup is beneficial, allowing you to deploy to preview first, evaluate how the site looks and behaves, and then proceed to deploy to production.

If you ever need to change the default production branch, you can do so in the Cloudflare dashboard under your Pages project > Settings > Builds & deployments > Configure Production deployments. At this stage, deploying to preview or production won't make much difference; everything will look and feel the same since it's a static website. However, when you incorporate an API with state, maintaining separate preview and production data becomes crucial.

You may not always want to deploy from your terminal, so in Chapter 14, Automate Workers & Pages Deployments, on page 193, you'll see other ways to deploy to Cloudflare, such as using Cloudflare's Git integration, or a GitHub Action.

That brings us to the end of another chapter; let's review.

What You've Learned

In this chapter, you learned how to build and deploy a static website to Cloudflare. Using npm create cloudflare, you created a new Pages project using the Next.js framework. You explored the important files in Next.js, and updated the default layout and page to contain the code needed for the weather application. Finally, you tested the application locally, and finished by deploying it to Cloudflare's global network.

This is just the start of the weather application. In the next chapter, you'll bring the weather application alive by introducing a back end that fetches live weather data from an external API.

Cloudflare Pages Limits

Similarly to Workers, Cloudflare Pages has limits built into the product too. On the free plan, you're limited to 500 deployments per month, with upgraded plans allowing a higher number per month. At the time of writing, a $20/month plan will unlock 5,000 builds per month.

Each project can contain up to 20,000 files, with the maximum file size for any given file being 25MiB.

You may think 20,000 might not be enough for larger content sites, but there are products available from Cloudflare to help move files out of your Pages project. In a later chapter, you'll take a look at Cloudflare's object storage product called R2, which hosts an unlimited number of files. In the event a lot of your files are assets, such as images, you would be able to move them out to R2 to reduce how many files are in your Pages project that's deployed to Cloudflare.

## CHAPTER 7

Add a Back End to the Front End

You now how to deploy a static application to Cloudflare using Next.js. It's an ideal approach for a simple website, such as a website for a business or landing pages. But most websites require some level of dynamic functionality. Even a blog, primarily consisting of static content, would benefit from features such as liking and commenting on posts, and subscribing to a newsletter.

Dynamic features such as those require a back end to handle data processing, and that's what you'll need for the weather application you're about to continue creating. You'll integrate a single API endpoint that will return weather information for a selected location to the front end. To do this, it'll fetch real-time data from Open-Meteo, a free, open-source weather API.[1]

As you've previously discovered in Chapter 2, Build a Serverless API, on page 11, deploying APIs to Cloudflare is possible using Workers. You could use the same approach to deploy an API separately to the Next.js application you're building, and simply call that API from Next.js. However, there's a downside; this method fragments your application code across two repositories, when, in reality, both are likely to change together.

This separation introduces a common challenge: what if you need to make breaking changes to your API? You'd find yourself performing a dance—updating the front end, deploying that change, then updating the back end, deploying the change, and likely circling back to tidy up the front end with yet another change and deployment.

That's all doable, there's an easier way. Next.js supports server-side routes. In a traditional setup, you'd run Next.js as a process and access the server-side routes it exposes. However, Cloudflare, being serverless, lacks a consistent running process. So, can you still leverage Next.js's server-side capabilities?

---

1. https://open-meteo.com/

The answer is yes, thanks to Cloudflare Pages Functions. These functions are crafted from server-side routes in Next.js, deployable as part of any Cloudflare Pages application. Essentially, they are a unique breed of Worker, specifically designed to run within a Cloudflare Pages project. Rather than creating a separate Worker, they're deployed from the same repository as the Cloudflare Pages project. This ensures the front end and back end remain synchronized, with changes localized to a single repository.

Before you look at Next.js specifically, let's look at how Functions work under the hood, as a lot of this detail is obscured when using Next.js. This approach works for other frameworks, such as Astro and Svelte—Cloudflare has specific adapters for those frameworks too.

Create a Pages Function

Creating a Pages Function is simple: First, create a new folder to house this very small server-side function; it should be completely separate to the weather app. I named mine cf-functions. Inside that folder, make a second folder called functions, and inside of the functions folder, create a file named hello.js and add the following code:

```
export function onRequest(context) {
  return new Response("Hey there!")
}
```

For this brief demonstration, I've opted for JavaScript instead of TypeScript to avoid additional dependencies. However, you can deploy Functions using TypeScript by using the .ts extension.

To create a straightforward endpoint handling a GET request, you export a function named onRequest that takes a single parameter called context. This context encompasses everything you'd expect, including details from the HTTP request and any dynamic URL parameters.

You also have access to the same ENV available when using Workers. It's accessible under context.ENV.your_binding_name, allowing you to bind various services to your Pages Function, like a D1 database. Binding services will be discussed in Chapter 8, Cache Data with KV, on page 97, as it's quite different from Workers.

For other HTTP request methods like POST, PUT, and PATCH, you append the HTTP verb to the end of the function name. For instance, to create a POST endpoint, export a function named onRequestPost. When using onRequest without any HTTP verbs, it gets called for any HTTP request, regardless of the HTTP method.

It's crucial that all these functions return an instance of Response from the Fetch API, mirroring the behavior of a Worker.

That's all you need to do. You can test it's working locally by running the following command in the root directory (e.g. in the cf-functions folder):

```
$ npx wrangler pages dev .
```

This will run your Pages project, with any static content under public being accessible (e.g. public/index.html would be the home page) and any Functions under the /functions directory are made available as server-side endpoints. Looking at the build output, you can see Cloudflare picked up the function and compiled it:

```
Compiling worker to "/tmp/functionsWorker-0.7228564482534758.mjs"...
Compiled Worker successfully

[mf:inf] Ready on http://127.0.0.1:8788/
```

The routing for Pages Functions uses the name of the file, minus the extension. Therefore, the endpoint you created is available under /hello. If you go to http://127.0.0.1:8788/hello (make sure you check the port in the output), you will see the Pages Function return the response defined in the onRequest function.

You can use folders to arrange your endpoints. If you wanted all the endpoints to be hosted under /api, you could move the hello.js file to /functions/api/hello.js and the endpoint would now be /api/hello.

You can also use dynamic path segments by wrapping the dynamic segment in square brackets. Let's say you're building out a comments API, and want to retrieve all comments for a given blog entry; you might create an API endpoint under /functions/api/comments/[blog_id].js.

Requests made to /api/comments/1 or /api/comments/some-blog-id would then hit that function, with the dynamic URL segment passed in the context parameter. As always, Cloudflare has extensive documentation on everything Pages Functions has to offer.[2]

As you'll be building the back end for the front end in Next.js, a lot of this will be obscured from you, but it's important to understand how Pages Functions works at a basic level before diving into the Next.js specifics. Now that you do, let's continue building your weather app.

---

2.   https://developers.cloudflare.com/pages/platform/functions/

Create a Serverless Next.js Route

While knowing how to create a basic server-side route with vanilla Cloudflare Pages Functions is useful, it's even more beneficial to build server-side routes within a comprehensive framework like Next.js. In the remainder of this chapter, you'll construct the endpoint necessary for fetching real-time weather forecasts and update the front end to display these forecasts.

The architecture is quite straightforward. You'll have the front end, featuring a list of available locations. Upon selecting a location, you'll be redirected to a dedicated page for that location. Subsequently, you'll retrieve and render the latest weather forecast for that specific location.

Cloudflare Pages seamlessly supports Next.js in edge mode, including server-side routes. This means you can write the routes just as you normally would in Next.js, and the @cloudflare/next-on-pages adapter will convert them at build time to function with Cloudflare.

This is incredibly beneficial, allowing you to write Next.js precisely as intended without worrying about deployment specifics. In reality, the application remains agnostic to where it's being deployed, at least in terms of the actual application code.

The first part you'll add is the server-side route that'll be responsible for retrieving the weather data from the Open-Meteo API. Add the following code to src/lib/get_external_weather_data.ts, making the lib directory in the process:

```
type OpenMeteoApiResponse = {
  current_weather: {
    temperature: Number,
    windspeed: Number
  }
}

const getExternalWeatherData = async(lat: Number, long: Number) => {
  const data_url = "https://api.open-meteo.com/v1/forecast" +
    `?latitude=${lat}&longitude=${long}&current_weather=true`

  return fetch(data_url)
    .then(response => response.json<OpenMeteoApiResponse>())
    .then(response => {
        return {
            temperature_celsius: response.current_weather.temperature,
            windspeed_kph: response.current_weather.windspeed
        }
    })
}

export default getExternalWeatherData;
```

As mentioned, you'll be using Open-Meteo's API for retrieving live weather information. The code above makes a call to their API, and wraps it in a simple function, which will be called from the API route in Next.js.

All this code does is call the API, passing in the latitude and longitude values of where you want to retrieve the weather from, and then return some of the fields. There's a lot more data available, so if you wanted to add the time in that location, the weather summary (e.g., sunny, cloudy, etc.) or the wind direction, you could.

As fetch returns a Promise, you can use method chaining to keep the code simple. The then method returns a Promise, so you're effectively chaining a series of Promises together, and each time one is resolved, the next handler that is defined is called.

In the above code, when a response is received from the API, it's parsed from JSON to an object. Once it's an object, some of the fields from the response are parsed out.

The Adapter Pattern

The getExternalWeatherData function is a simple wrapper around an API call, effectively implementing the adapter pattern.

The Adapter pattern is useful when communicating with external services, keeping the core of your application decoupled from any outside services or incompatible interfaces. In this case, you're converting the response from the Open-Meteo API into an object that is passed back to the rest of the application.

The result is the rest of the application doesn't know anything about this API call, or that calls are being made to Open-Meteo, as all it sees is the response object returned. The API could be changed from Open-Meteo to another weather API, and the rest of the application wouldn't know nor be affected, as the adapter would just be updated to call a different API, but return the same object. This function could even retrieve static data, and as long as the response is in the same format, the rest of the application wouldn't know the source of the data.

The Adapter pattern isn't only used with APIs; you could use it to wrap a call to an external npm library for example. Perhaps that library returns an ArrayBuffer, and rather than having to deal with parsing that every time you need to use that library, you wrap the calls to that library and handle the conversion in an adapter.

You now have the ability to retrieve external weather information, so let's add the server-side route to the Next.js application. Add the following to src/app/api/weather/route.ts, creating the new folders as necessary:

```
import getExternalWeatherData from "@/lib/get_external_weather_data";

export const runtime = 'edge';

const countries = [
  {
    country: "london",
    title: "London, UK",
    lat: 51.50853,
    long: -0.12574
  },
  {
    country: "new-york",
    title: "New York, US",
    lat: 40.71427,
    long: -74.00597
  },
  {
    country: "los-angeles",
    title: "Los Angeles, US",
    lat: 34.05223,
    long: -118.24368
  },
  {
    country: "berlin",
    title: "Berlin, Germany",
    lat: 52.52437,
    long: 13.41053
  },
  {
    country: "tokyo",
    title: "Tokyo, Japan",
    lat: 35.6895,
    long: 139.69171
  }
]

export async function GET(request: Request) {
  const request_url = new URL(request.url)
  const requested_country = request_url.searchParams.get('country')
  const country_config = countries.find(
    (c) => c.country == requested_country
  )

  if (!country_config) {
    return new Response('You must provide a valid country', { status: 404})
  }

  let weather_data = await getExternalWeatherData(
```

```
    country_config.lat,
    country_config.long
  );

  const response = {
    temperature_celsius: weather_data.temperature_celsius,
    windspeed_kph: weather_data.windspeed_kph,
    title: country_config.title
  }
  return new Response(JSON.stringify(response), {
    headers: { 'content-type': 'application/json' }
  });
}
```

There are quite a few lines of code here, so let's walk through it section by section.

First, the function you just created is imported, and this server-side route is defined as an edge endpoint.

In Chapter 6, Build a Static Website with Pages, on page 65, you learned the different runtime options available for Next.js. Here, you can see that the endpoint has been configured for the edge runtime, so that during build, Next.js understands what runtime the application will be deployed to, and it can format the project accordingly. Its build is even clever enough to notify you of problems before deployment, such as using a Node library that isn't available in the edge runtime.

Second, a list of available locations is defined. This is the same list you used in the select element in the front end. The Open-Meteo API works based on latitude and longitude coordinates, so you need to map the locations to their latitude and longitude.

To make it easier to add other locations in the future, it would be wise to store these in a database, and have both the weather look up and front end use the data in the database, but for this simple application, this works perfectly well.

With the configuration complete, you can define the method that will be called when the server-side endpoint is hit with a request. In Next.js, server-side route names map to HTTP verbs. You can define all the types you'd expect, including GET, POST, PATCH, PUT, and DELETE.

In this case, the front end will be retrieving data from this endpoint, so you define a GET function, which gets passed a Request object. You then use that request object to extract the data needed:

```
const request_url = new URL(request.url)
const requested_country = request_url.searchParams.get('country')
const country_config = countries.find(
  (c) => c.country == requested_country
)
```

The request URL will be something like localhost:8788/api/weather?country=london. The application needs the country query string parameter, so that's extracted on the second line.

Now that you know what location has been selected on the front end, you can retrieve the configuration for that location, as you need the latitude and longitude values. With those values, you can call the Open-Meteo API:

```
if (!country_config) {
  return new Response('You must provide a valid country', { status: 404})
}

let weather_data = await getExternalWeatherData(
  country_config.lat,
  country_config.long
);
```

There's some simple error handling in the event the requested location can't be found, in which case a 404 is returned. Assuming the country has been found, you then use the getExternalWeatherData function that calls the Open-Meteo API, passing it the latitude and longitude values based on the location selected.

Lastly, a response is returned:

```
const response = {
  temperature_celsius: weather_data.temperature_celsius,
  windspeed_kph: weather_data.windspeed_kph,
  title: country_config.title
}

return new Response(JSON.stringify(response), {
  headers: { 'content-type': 'application/json' }
});
```

You could return the response from the getExternalWeatherData as-is, except the front end is going to show a title for the location selected, so that is added to the response before it's returned.

That's all there is to the server-side endpoint, so let's check it's working as expected.

Test the Server-Side Endpoint

Before you move on to implementing the front end changes needed to call the server-side route, you can check the route you added works in isolation. In your terminal, run the following command, making sure you're in the weather-app folder:

```
npm run dev
```

Once Next.js starts, head over to your browser and type in the following:

```
http://localhost:3000/api/weather?country=london
```

All being well, you should see a response that looks something like this:

```
{"temperature_celsius":20.9,"windspeed_kph":6.2,"title":"London, UK"}
```

Luckily for me, at the time of writing, it was a beautiful, warm day in London!

With the server-side route working, you can move on to updating the front end, which will call the server-side route and render the data in a prettier format.

Call the Server-Side Route from the Front End

Before making the call to the server-side route from the front end, let's understand the changes you need to implement.

Currently, there's a single page, the home page, showcasing the select field and some hardcoded weather data for New York. The first step is to remove the hardcoded weather data, leaving only the select field on the home page. Following this, you'll create a new page incorporating a dynamic parameter for the selected location, resembling something like /weather/london.

Upon selecting a location from the field, you'll utilize that location to redirect users to the appropriate URL. The responsibility of this new page is to fetch live weather data from the server-side route and render it.

To make the front end a little tidier, you'll begin breaking it into components. This practice is common in React, where, in larger projects, reusable components are crucial. Even in smaller projects, it's a useful way to isolate sections of the front end, facilitating independent development and testing.

You'll add one component for the button on the home page, with the code going in src/components/Button/index.tsx (on the next page).

```
'use client';

import { useRouter } from 'next/navigation'

export const Button = () => {
  const router = useRouter();

  function handleClick() {
    let location = document.getElementById(
      'location-select'
    ) as unknown as HTMLSelectElement;

    router.push(`/weather/${location.value}`)
  }

  return (
    <a href="#"
      type="button"
      style={{textDecoration: 'none'}}
      onClick={handleClick}
    >
      <span className="input-group-text border-0 fw-bold"
          id="search-addon"
          style={{background: 'none'}}
      >
        Check!
      </span>
    </a>
  )
}
```

At the top, 'use client' is there to tell Next.js this is a client-side component, primarily because you need to use onClick on the link to trigger some client-side code to redirect the user. Without this directive at the top, Next.js would refuse to build the component, as by default, Next.js will treat these as server-side components where functions such as onClick are not available.

There's nothing too complex in this component; it's simply rendering a button that, when clicked, will redirect to a location-specific page based on what's selected in the select field. Due to some TypeScript quirks, you have to double-cast the select element to keep the type checking happy. You can remove the as unknown part, and the application will run fine, but you'll get warnings in the build output.

The second component you need to add is for the weather information that will be showing on that location-specific page; it needs to go in src/components/WeatherInfo/index.tsx:

```
import PropTypes from "prop-types";

type WeatherInfoProps = {
  location: String,
  temperature: Number,
  windspeed: Number
}

export const WeatherInfo = (
  {location, temperature, windspeed}: WeatherInfoProps
) => {
  return (
    <div className="card shadow-0 border">
      <div className="card-body p-4">
        <h4 className="mb-1 sfw-normal">
            {location}
        </h4>
        <p className="mb-2">
          Current temperature: <strong>{temperature.toString()}°C</strong>
        </p>
        <p className="mb-2">
          Windspeed: <strong>{windspeed.toString()}kph</strong>
        </p>
      </div>
    </div>
  )
}

WeatherInfo.propTypes = {
  location: PropTypes.string.isRequired,
  temperature: PropTypes.number.isRequired,
  windspeed: PropTypes.number.isRequired
}
```

This component is even simpler than the button, as it's just rendering a few HTML elements that will show the weather information. It accepts some parameters, location, temperature, and windspeed, and uses those to render the information. When defining a component, you can use PropTypes to define the properties that component accepts. When you use the component in a page, you'll see the parameters passed.

Before you create the location-specific page, you need to remove the hardcoded weather information from the home page, as well as use your new button component.

As you'll be introducing a second page, and you want all the pages to have the same centralized style, you first need to move the consistent wrapper that will be present on every page to the root layout. Open src/app/layout.tsx and update the RootLayout function to the code on the following page:

```
export default function RootLayout({
  children,
}: {
  children: React.ReactNode
}) {
  return (
    <html lang="en">
      <body className={inter.className}>
        <section className="vh-100">
          <div className="container py-5 h-100">

            <div className="row d-flex justify-content-center
                align-items-center h-100">
              <div className="col-md-8 col-lg-6 col-xl-4">
                {children}
              </div>
            </div>
          </div>
        </section>
      </body>
    </html>
  )
}
```

Now you need to remove the hardcoded weather information from the home page, and make use of the Button component by updating src/app/page.tsx:

```
import { Button } from "@/components/Button"

export default function Home() {
  return (
    <div className="home-body">

      <h3 className="mb-4 pb-2 fw-normal">Check the weather forecast</h3>

      <div className="input-group rounded mb-3">
        <select className="form-control rounded" aria-label="Search"
          aria-describedby="search-addon" id="location-select">
          <option value="london">London, UK</option>
          <option value="new-york">New York, US</option>
          <option value="los-angeles">Los Angeles, US</option>
          <option value="berlin">Berlin, Germany</option>
          <option value="tokyo">Tokyo, Japan</option>
        </select>

        <Button />
      </div>
    </div>
  )
}
```

The only change here was to remove the HTML that was centralizing the page information, as that's now been moved to the layout, and render the button using the component you created. To render the button component, you must import it at the top, and then you can use it like any other JSX element.

With the housekeeping done, you can finally add the new page that will render dynamic weather information based on the location selected. In the file path below, it's worth noting the square brackets. In Next.js, this is how you define dynamic routes, where the part in the square brackets is a dynamic URL segment. For this page, any requests to /weather/london or /weather/berlin will use this page. You can add as many parameters as you need.

For now, you'll just need one parameter, though. Add the following code to src/app/weather/[location]/page.tsx, creating the folders as necessary:

```tsx
'use client';

import { WeatherInfo } from "@/components/WeatherInfo"
import { useEffect, useState } from "react";
import Link from 'next/link'

type Weather = {
  location: String,
  temperature: Number,
  windspeed: Number
}

type WeatherApiResponse = {
  title: String,
  temperature_celsius: Number,
  windspeed_kph: Number
}

export const runtime = 'edge';

export default function Page({ params }: { params: { location: string } }) {
  const [weatherData, setWeatherData] = useState<Weather | null>(null);
  useEffect(() => {
    fetch(`/api/weather?country=${params.location}`)
        .then(response => response.json<WeatherApiResponse>())
        .then(response => setWeatherData({
            location: response.title,
            temperature: response.temperature_celsius,
            windspeed: response.windspeed_kph
          })
        )
  }, [params.location]);
  return (
    <>
      {weatherData && (
        <>
          <div id="weather-info">
            <WeatherInfo location={weatherData.location}
                         temperature={weatherData.temperature}
```

```
                        windspeed={weatherData.windspeed}
          />
        </div>
        <Link href="/">Back</Link>
      </>
    )}

    {!weatherData && (
        <div>
          <h3 id="loading-text">Loading...</h3>
        </div>
      )}
    </>
  )
}
```

With a few moving parts in this code, let's step through it slowly. Firstly, a couple of types are defined that represent the weather information that will be shown, and the response format from the API route you created. There's also some state needed for this page:

```
type Weather = {
  location: String,
  temperature: Number,
  windspeed: Number
}
type WeatherApiResponse = {
  title: String,
  temperature_celsius: Number,
  windspeed_kph: Number
}
export const runtime = 'edge';

export default function Page({ params }: { params: { location: string } }) {
  const [weatherData, setWeatherData] = useState<Weather | null>(null);
```

Using useState, you can manage and retrieve state specific to a component. This state persists as long as the component is rendered in the browser, making it handy for storing data persistently required by the component. For instance, imagine a simple counter increasing by 1 each time you press a button—you could efficiently store the state for that counter with useState, and any updates to the counter would be reflected in the front end.

The other important line here is the export of the runtime constant. This informs Next.js and Cloudflare that this is an edge route, indicating it should execute on the server side, not the client side.

You can access the data stored in the component's state through weatherData, and set it with setWeatherData. Now that there's a place to store and retrieve the data essential for the component, you can proceed to implement the logic for fetching data from the server-side endpoint:

```
useEffect(() => {
  fetch(`/api/weather?country=${params.location}`)
      .then(response => response.json<WeatherApiResponse>())
      .then(response => setWeatherData({
            location: response.title,
            temperature: response.temperature_celsius,
            windspeed: response.windspeed_kph
          })
      )
}, [params.location]);
```

Similarly to before, you are using method chaining with fetch. You query the server-side route you created for the location using the location passed in the query string. Once you've received the response, you parse the JSON into an object, and then set the data in the state.

This is all wrapped in useEffect, a React hookwhich lets you include side effects in your components and pages by providing a way to add supplementary logic to a component. By default, it's invoked on each render. The second parameter, where [params.location] is passed, specifies what must change for this hook to execute.

Lastly, you render the content you want to show on the front end:

```
return (
  <>
    {weatherData && (
      <>
        <div id="weather-info">
          <WeatherInfo location={weatherData.location}
                       temperature={weatherData.temperature}
                       windspeed={weatherData.windspeed}
          />
        </div>
        <Link href="/">Back</Link>
      </>
    )}

    {!weatherData && (
        <div>
          <h3 id="loading-text">Loading...</h3>
        </div>
    )}
  </>
)
```

As the state is held in weatherData, you can change the view based on this state. You do so by providing a conditional statement in curly braces, and then defining the JSX you want to render if that conditional is true inside regular brackets. If the condition is met, the JSX will be rendered, or else it won't be rendered.

If weather data is returned, you render the information for the given location. If you don't, you render some loading text while the API call completes.

That's all the changes made; let's look at what the weather looks like in the world today by running the application locally!

Run the Weather App Locally

As you are still working with a standard Next.js application, with a sprinkling of Cloudflare magic at build time, local development is still as easy as running npm run dev.

Once the application starts, navigate to localhost:3000 (always verify the port in the terminal), and you'll see the home page, now featuring only a select field.

Choose a location, press the check button, and you'll be redirected to the location-specific page, presenting real-time weather data. Go back, choose another location, and the weather for that location will be displayed instead.

Deploy a Pages Application

If you'd like to deploy the application to Cloudflare to make sure it's all working in production, simply run npm run deploy and follow the prompts. You'll want to create a new project, and use whatever branch you merge all your code into for your production branch (e.g., master or main).

Once deployed, you can open the URL given to you, which will look something like https://xxxx.weather-test-123.pages.dev. It may take a few minutes for the DNS to propagate, so don't be concerned if you get SSL or DNS errors initially.

Before April 2024, Pages projects didn't support wrangler.toml to manage deployments. If you remember from Chapter 4, Persist Data with D1, on page 33, wrangler.toml is used to manage key Cloudflare-specific configuration, such as bindings. You can also modify compatibility flags, which allow you to tweak the runtime that your application runs in.

Given that the application runs on Cloudflare in the V8 runtime—similar to the Chrome browser—you don't have access to any Node modules by default.

As Next.js relies on certain Node modules to function, and numerous npm packages utilize Node modules, Cloudflare is progressively incorporating select Node modules into the runtime.

At the time of writing, the following Node modules are available in Cloudflare's runtime:

- assert
- AsyncLocalStorage
- Buffer
- Crypto
- Diagnostics Channel
- EventEmitter
- path
- process
- Streams
- StringDecoder
- util

Cloudflare is regularly adding more Node modules, and I suspect eventually there will be complete support for Node.

By default, these modules are not included in the runtime. To opt-in, you need to set a compatibility flag. If you take a look at wrangler.toml, you'll see the following:

```
compatibility_flags = ["nodejs_compat"]
```

As you're using C3 to create projects, it does a lot of the heavy lifting for you. Cloudflare knows that Next.js needs some additional Node modules, so it's configured wrangler.toml accordingly. In this case, it's added the nodejs_compat flag, which makes the Node modules above available for use.

What You've Learned

You've now taken what was a static website and added back end functionality to it by adding server-side routes to a Next.js application. During the build process, these are transformed into Cloudflare Pages Functions, which are effectively Cloudflare Workers, operating in a serverless environment.

You also learned how to test those server-side routes and deploy them.

We have one more chapter to go on building full-stack applications. So far, you've made exclusive use of the Next.js edge runtime to run an application in a serverless way. It's working nicely, but if you refresh the weather page for a country several times, you'll notice it breaks after a while.

This is because the Open-Meteo API has a relatively small rate limit, unless you purchase a premium plan. In the next chapter, you'll use another Cloudflare service called KV to get around this problem by caching the weather data rather than repeatedly making API calls.

## CHAPTER 8

Cache Data with KV

Your weather application has evolved into a fully-fledged full-stack application, with the front end and back end deployed together within the same application. Successful integration with Open-Meteo's API on the back end has enabled the dynamic rendering of front end components for users accessing the application.

Now, picture deploying this application to production and sharing the link with all your friends, and to anyone with internet access.

Oops! Some of them run into error pages. On investigation, it becomes apparent that the API calls to Open-Meteo are failing due to rate limits. It's a potential disaster, rendering the website unusable for anyone.

Fortunately, there are well-established solutions for such issues. While a premium plan with Open-Meteo is an option, costing 30 euros per month, there's a more economical approach given the current support for only five locations and the relatively slow rate of weather changes. The solution is to cache the response from the Open-Meteo API for a specified duration—let's say an hour. This approach limits API calls to a maximum of five times per hour (one per location), preventing the application from hitting API rate limits, and enhancing performance and reliability.

The performance gains stem from the fact that retrieving data from a cache is typically much faster than making an API call. Caches are designed to respond rapidly, often within a few milliseconds. Additionally, reliability improves since the responsiveness of Open-Meteo's API cannot be guaranteed. Intermittent failures or outages may occur, causing the weather application to fail to return weather data. Leveraging a cache reduces the likelihood of such failures, as the application interacts with a simple cache hosted within Cloudflare, avoiding external network calls to a third-party API.

So, let's enhance the weather API route of the weather application to cache data fetched from the Open-Meteo API. The approach involves checking the cache for data before making an external API call to Open-Meteo, which you'll do by using a product from Cloudflare called KV.

Create a New KV Namespace

Although you could use a popular distributed cache like Redis or Memcached, Cloudflare offers its own cache, known as KV, tailored to work seamlessly with its developer platform.

KV is a global, low-latency, key-value data store. It stores data in a small number of centralized data centers, then caches that data close to your users, in Cloudflare's data centers, when data is requested. We'll get into the specifics of KV and some of its nuances as we go through the chapter.

Now that you understand what KV is and what we aim to achieve, let's start by creating the cache.

Similar to all the services used so far, KV is serverless. No underlying infrastructure management is required—no servers to create, no maintenance concerns, and no worries regarding whether this cache will handle the required throughput.

Therefore, creating a cache for any application is incredibly simple, and can be done by executing the following two commands:

```
$ npx wrangler kv namespace create WEATHER_CACHE
$ npx wrangler kv namespace create WEATHER_CACHE_PREVIEW
```

When developing on Pages, there are two environments: production and preview. Production is exactly what it sounds like; it's the environment that your end users would use. Preview can be used to test changes before pushing to production, with its own set of resources. One branch will be designated your production branch, and any other branch that's deployed will be deployed to preview.

Executing the two commands will result in two KV namespaces being created—one designated for production, and the other for preview. Although it's technically possible to use the same KV namespace for both production and preview, adhering to best practices involves maintaining strict separation between the two environments. This approach ensures that we can't accidentally impact production data while developing the application.

Here's the output you'll see once the namespace has been created:

```
wrangler 3.25.0
-------------------------------------------------------
Creating namespace with title "weather-app-WEATHER_CACHE"

Success!
Add the following to your configuration file in your kv_namespaces array:
{ binding = "WEATHER_CACHE", id = "2bc7ad8e738644f88056b8a3902b8528" }
```

As you can see, a new KV namespace has been created.

Some additional changes are needed to bind resources to a Pages project versus a Worker, so let's dive into how to bind a KV namespace to a Pages project.

Bind KV Namespaces

In Chapter 4, Persist Data with D1, on page 33, the wrangler.toml file was used to bind a D1 database to a Worker. By default, the same file is used in Pages projects to configure any bindings. Alternatively, you can define the bindings manually in the Cloudflare dashboard, but I would always recommend using wrangler.toml as it keeps the configuration for your application under version control.

By default, Cloudflare will create a wrangler.toml file in the root of any new Pages project configured to be a source of truth for any bindings for that project. In essence, if pages_build_output_dir is set in that file, it'll be used to define any bindings.

For local development, any bindings need to go at the top of wrangler.toml. You need to add your KV namespace to that by adding the following:

```
[[kv_namespaces]]
binding = "WEATHER_CACHE"
id = "xxx"
preview_id = "yyy"
```

For the id and preview_id field, you need to use the ID for the preview KV namespace you created above. As this file is only used for local development, you could complete the id field, but if you want to test remotely in Cloudflare's sandbox mode, you'll need to provide a preview_id. When running an application on Cloudflare's servers, it'll use the real KV namespace, whereas locally it'll simulate a KV namespace on your local machine.

The wrangler.toml file has the concept of environments, allowing you to define environment-specific configuration. To define resources for preview and production, add the following to wrangler.toml:

```
[[env.preview.kv_namespaces]]
binding = "WEATHER_CACHE"
id = "xxx"

[[env.production.kv_namespaces]]
binding = "WEATHER_CACHE"
id = "yyy"
```

You need to replace xxx with the ID of the preview KV namespace, and replace yyy with the ID of the production KV namespace.

For local development, Cloudflare will use the top-level kv_namespaces binding, for preview it'll use env.preview.kv_namespaces, and for production it'll use env.production.kv_namespaces.

With the KV namespaces bound to the weather application, you can move on to use KV within the weather application.

Cache Data in KV

Before you implement KV, understanding how KV works is crucial, especially given its distinct characteristics compared to other distributed caches you might have encountered. If you've used a distributed cache before like Redis, you're likely familiar with single-digit latency and may have been involved in managing the underlying infrastructure or setting up a Redis cluster.

Typically, applications interacting with Redis are geographically close. For instance, you might host an application on EC2, and it communicates with a Redis cluster also hosted in AWS. This proximity ensures consistently low latency, often in the single-digit milliseconds.

Now, when it comes to Cloudflare, we're in a different realm altogether—we're at the edge. Any request to an application is served from the nearest data center to the user, significantly reducing latency compared to hosting your application on an EC2 instance. This is a substantial advantage for the edge, resulting in more responsive websites and shorter loading times for end users.

However, this approach introduces its own set of challenges. Understanding how KV operates is important to grasp these challenges. When a Cloudflare Worker handles a request—and remember that Pages uses Workers under the hood—Cloudflare loads your Worker into memory at the closest available data center to the request and processes the request there. Everything occurs on Cloudflare's edge servers.

With KV, central data centers are responsible for storing the data. When you write to KV, you're essentially writing to a central data store, and that write is replicated to other central data stores. However, KV operates on an eventually-consistent model, meaning a write to KV may take up to sixty seconds to be globally available across Cloudflare's network. This delay is a trade-off for the benefits of edge computing.

Eventual Consistency

In distributed systems, there are several types of consistency when it comes to data. When talking about KV, it is eventually-consistent, which means that eventually all reads for a given piece of data will return the most up-to-date value.

By definition, that means for a period of time, you could make two reads for the same key in KV, and be returned different values for each read request. It can vary from product to product, but one of the primary reasons for this happening is when data is updated, it takes time to propagate.

In the case of KV, we know that there are centralized data centers where the data in KV is ultimately stored, and we also know that data from KV can be cached in many places across the Cloudflare network, such as on the edge servers. When you write to KV, you write to the centralized data centers, and it can take up to 60 seconds for that data to be updated in all the places it exists, as it gradually propagates around the network, therefore making it eventually consistent.

For completeness, the opposite of eventual consistency is strong consistency, where the data returned is always guaranteed to be the most up-to-date information.

These data stores are centralized, meaning they don't handle requests at the edge. When a Worker gets a request and needs to read a value from KV, it checks if it has the info cached on the edge server. If it does, great—it returns it. If not, it tries to get it from the central data center cache, and if that fails, it goes to disk from the central data store. Picture it like tiers: best reads from the regional edge, worst from the central store.

There might be other tiers, but KV aims for the most efficient way, ideally from cached data in a data center's memory, rather than fetching it from disk. Here's the scenario for the worst-performing read, where the data has to come from the central data store:

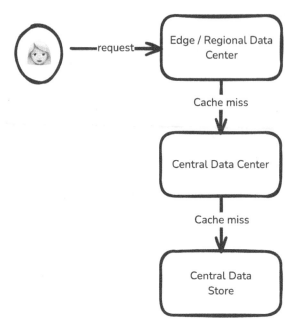

It's worth noting writes will trigger purges across Cloudflare's network within seconds to ensure any keys held in KV that are updated or deleted are removed from caches, forcing KV to retrieve the most up-to-date value from the central data store. This happens in the background, though, with KV working to ensure requests are always handled in the most optimal way possible.

By design, KV is intended for use with high-read applications, particularly where you can cache the data for a while and get a lot of value out of that value being cached. If you're constantly writing to KV, or reading very little, you won't see much benefit from using KV. That doesn't mean it can't be used for low-traffic applications, or in cases where you simply can't hit the non-cached value too often, such as your use case here, but you'll get the most value from using it on high-read applications.

Now, armed with the nitty-gritty of how KV works, let's slot it into the weather app. It's a perfect match here, as the app needs to prevent too many calls to the Open-Meteo API, and it can happily cache weather data for a good while, as weather info doesn't change every other minute.

The first change you need to make is to ensure that Cloudflare knows to expect the KV namespace to be present in its environment. When the application was bootstrapped using npm create cloudflare, it'll have created a env.d.ts file in the root of the project, open it and update the CloudflareEnv interface to include the KV namespace:

```
interface CloudflareEnv {
  WEATHER_CACHE: KVNamespace;
}
```

This defines an interface for Cloudflare's runtime environment, and defines WEATHER_CACHE with the type of KVNamespace.

Just as Cloudflare Workers get injected with bindings on the fly, the same goes for Cloudflare Pages. The twist? Every framework handles its environment differently. For Next.js, Cloudflare has built tooling that simplifies this for you—along with other popular frameworks too. With a little bit of setup, you'll have full access to bindings locally.

With the KVNamespace you want to use configured for local development, you can update the server-side API route to handle caching.

Open src/app/api/weather/route.ts and update the GET endpoint to the following:

```
import getExternalWeatherData from "@/lib/get_external_weather_data";

export const runtime = 'edge';

const countries = [
  {
    country: "london",
    title: "London, UK",
    lat: 51.50853,
    long: -0.12574
  },
  {
    country: "new-york",
    title: "New York, US",
    lat: 40.71427,
    long: -74.00597
  },
  {
    country: "los-angeles",
    title: "Los Angeles, US",
    lat: 34.05223,
    long: -118.24368
  },
  {
    country: "berlin",
    title: "Berlin, Germany",
    lat: 52.52437,
    long: 13.41053
  },
  {
    country: "tokyo",
    title: "Tokyo, Japan",
    lat: 35.6895,
```

```
      long: 139.69171
   }
]

import { getRequestContext } from '@cloudflare/next-on-pages'

export async function GET(request: Request) {
  const cache = getRequestContext().env.WEATHER_CACHE;
  const request_url = new URL(request.url)
  const requested_country = request_url.searchParams.get('country')
  const country_config = countries.find(
    (c) => c.country == requested_country
  )

  if (!country_config) {
    return new Response(
      'You must provide a valid country',
      { status: 404}
    )
  }

  const cached_data = await cache.get(
    `location:${requested_country}`
  );

  let weather_data;

  if (!cached_data) {
    console.log("No cached data found")

    weather_data = await getExternalWeatherData(
      country_config.lat,
      country_config.long
    );

    await cache.put(
      `location:${requested_country}`,
      JSON.stringify(weather_data),
      { expirationTtl: 3600 } // 1 hour
    );
  } else {
    console.log("Cached data found");

    weather_data = JSON.parse(cached_data)
  }

  const response = {
    temperature_celsius: weather_data.temperature_celsius,
    windspeed_kph: weather_data.windspeed_kph,
    title: country_config.title
  }

  return new Response(JSON.stringify(response), {
    headers: { 'content-type': 'application/json' }
  });
}
```

Quite a few lines have been added to this function, and instead of a single line of code that was making a call to the Open-Meteo API, you now have to handle the cache. Let's break it down into sections.

You start by importing and using a helper function, provided by Cloudflare's Next.js-specific adapter:

```
import { getRequestContext } from '@cloudflare/next on pages'

export async function GET(request: Request) {
  const cache = getRequestContext().env.WEATHER_CACHE;
```

Whenever you want to retrieve a binding in a Cloudflare Pages project, you must use getRequestContext().env.BINDING_NAME. Behind the scenes, Cloudflare will load the appropriate binding, irrespective of whether you're running locally or on Cloudflare's servers. This allows you to use npm run dev and still have access to your bindings locally.

Next, you try to retrieve some data from the cache:

```
const cached_data = await cache.get(
  `location:${requested_country}`
);

let weather_data;
```

The first line is simple enough, it defines a variable that will be populated later with the final result to return from the API. The second line is making a call to the KV namespace you created earlier.

In this case, it'll inject WEATHER_CACHE into the environment at runtime, along with any other services you've bound to the Pages project. Interacting with Cloudflare services is made easy too, as a fully-featured client that exposes methods for you to use is injected at runtime.

There are four available to use:

- get to retrieve data
- put to write data
- delete to remove data
- list to list the keys stored in KV

You'll be using the first two in this application.

KV, being a key-value store, keeps things wonderfully simple. Each entry has a key and a value, and no two entries share the same key. Write to an existing key? It gets overwritten.

When you're fetching data, just give it the key. Here, the key has a prefix of location: followed by the requested location. Since key-value stores don't bother with tables or collections, it's common to use prefixes to flag the type of data a key relates to.

Alternatively, as you pay for what you use on Cloudflare, you could create a separate KV namespace for each data set. If you require a cache in two different parts of your application, I'd probably create two KV namespaces, whereas if you needed to cache two separate types of data in the same area, I'd probably use one. The decision very much depends on the context, so you'll need to make the best decision for your use case.

After attempting to retrieve the data from KV, the application needs to check whether the cache hit was successful or not:

```
if (!cached_data) {
  console.log("No cached data found")

  weather_data = await getExternalWeatherData(
    country_config.lat,
    country_config.long
  );

  await cache.put(
    `location:${requested_country}`,
    JSON.stringify(weather_data),
    { expirationTtl: 3600 } // 1 hour
  );
```

Data is stored in KV as a string, so if a value is found for the given key in the cache, it'll return a string; otherwise, it'll return null.

If no cached data was returned, a log entry is created that no cached data was found, and then an API call to Open-Meteo is made by calling the getExternalWeatherData function.

Once the weather data has been returned from the API, the application can then cache that data in KV by calling put, which is used to write data to KV. You pass three parameters: the first is the key to store the data under, the second is the value you want to store, and the third is passing expirationTTl, which is the number of seconds to cache the key for. In this case, the application will cache the weather data for an hour before its value is purged from the cache.

Alternatively to the expirationTtl, you can pass expiration, which achieves the same outcome of expiring a key, but you need to pass the number of seconds since the epoch instead.

Another useful parameter is metadata, allowing you to store additional key-value pairs that relate to the data you're storing. Let's say the weather application evolves, and you want a backup data source alongside the Open-Meteo API. To differentiate in the cache between which source was used, you could store that as metadata, and use that when rendering the weather data to inform the user what the source of the data was.

As the value in KV is stored as a string, we have to serialize the weather data using JSON.stringify before writing it to KV.

Lastly, the scenario where cached data was returned from KV is handled:

```
} else {
  console.log("Cached data found");
  weather_data = JSON.parse(cached_data)
}
```

Just like logging when you don't find cached data, it's handy to log when you do. Since the front end stays indifferent to whether data comes from the cache or not, logging helps you ensure your code dances to the expected tune.

In KV, values are stored as strings. When you wrote to KV, you serialized the object holding the weather data. Now, when you read from KV, use JSON.parse to deserialize. You can store non-JSON values too, such as strings.

The rest of the code is unchanged from before, with the weather data being returned in the response to the front end.

And there you have it—those are the tweaks for caching with KV. It's a small change, but it packs a punch in application performance. Imagine if people repeatedly asked for the weather in a certain country; KV would be the hero, boosting performance.

For this app, the cache has a higher chance of getting hits. Why? Users are likely asking for their local weather. KV works its magic on the edge, caching data there. So, if the London users want weather info, they all likely hit the same edge server, resulting in more cache hits.

That's the superpower of edge computing: keeping requests and data right where the end users are.

With the weather application now caching weather data, let's test everything is working as expected locally, before deploying to production.

Test the Caching Locally

When you rolled out the caching logic, you smartly threw in some logging for good measure. Since the app looks the same to end users, cache or no cache, that logging is our key to know if the cache is being used or not.

You need to run npm run dev to start the weather application. Once the command has finished, press b to open the application in your browser, and select a location to view the weather for. If you take a look in your terminal, you'll see the requests logged, along with any custom logs that are written using console.log:

```
[mf:inf] GET /api/weather 200 OK (357ms)
[mf:inf] GET /weather/los-angeles 200 OK (67ms)
No cached data found
```

As this is the first time any weather data has been requested since you introduced KV, there's naturally no cache data, and that's reflected in the logs. If you were to then select the same country again, you'd see the following output:

```
[mf:inf] GET /weather/los-angeles 200 OK (67ms)
Cached data found
```

If you repeat the same for another country, you'll see each time that the first request is retrieved from the API, and subsequent requests are retrieved from the cache.

React Strict Mode

 You might wonder why you see logs being produced twice per page render, and that's because of React's strict mode. In short, it double renders each page in development to help you try to find problems with your components. You can disable it by setting reactStrictMode to false in next.config.mjs. Strict mode is only enabled in development, so you won't see this behavior in production.

Here's the cool part: stop the app, restart it, and the data still pops up from the cache. Behind the scenes, all the local simulation is handled by Miniflare, an npm package from Cloudflare. Miniflare is simulating the same environment that Workers, and their supporting services such as KV, run in when deployed to Cloudflare. As Cloudflare Pages effectively runs on Workers, the local emulation is needed here too.

When data is stored in KV, it's written into the root folder where your application runs, named .wrangler. You can see data being stored locally by looking in .wrangler/state/v3/kv/ from the root of the project, and it'll show you some files that are being used to store any data held in your cache. The folder name may vary between operating systems, but at present the ID of your KV namespace is used.

You won't want to commit this data to version control, so make sure for all your projects you add an ignore rule that prevents .wrangler being committed. If you want to remove any data held in the cache, you can safely delete the .wrangler folder at any time.

With the application working locally, you can deploy to Cloudflare and see how the application performs on actual Cloudflare servers.

Deploy to Cloudflare

There are no changes from the last chapter in terms of deployment, so you can simply run npm run deploy to deploy the weather application to Cloudflare. If you're making your changes on the production branch (e.g., main or master) it'll be deployed to production, else it'll be deployed to preview.

Once deployed, don't view the application yet at the URL; that's output in the terminal.

When you were testing locally, you were able to confirm the cache was being used from the logs. You can do the same when the application is deployed to Cloudflare, albeit it from the Cloudflare dashboard.

Go to Workers & Pages, and click the project for the weather application. It'll take you to a list of deployments, click view details on the most recent one. On the next page, select Functions from the submenu and scroll down until you see Real-time logs.

Real-time logs allow you to see logs from your applications for each request that is handled. Not only will it show any logs produced while handling that request, it'll show other information such as the status code and some HTTP headers. I use this all the time to debug issues in production, as it'll also log any exceptions that occur during the execution of your code.

Click the Begin log stream button, and after a few seconds, you'll see a message informing you the page is listening for new events.

If you now open the URL for your deployed application from your terminal and navigate through the website, you'll see logs appear on this page in real time. You can click on each one for more information, including the logs indicating whether the cache was hit or not.

Alongside the logs, we can view the data stored in KV in the Cloudflare dashboard too. On the left menu, under Workers & Pages, click KV, and then click the view link next to the KV namespace you created.

Once the page loads, you'll be able to see all the key-value pairs stored in that KV namespace.

If you want to verify the preview configuration is working as expected too, simply create a new branch locally (git checkout -b test-preview) and run npm run deploy again. You'll notice in the dashboard, under your project, that this deploy is marked as preview, and you'll notice the data goes into the preview KV namespace instead.

Persistent logs are not available for Pages projects, but they are for Workers, which will be covered in View and Query Logs, on page 219. Before recapping what you've learned in this chapter, let's take a look at the limits for KV.[1]

Limit Type	Free Tier	Paid Tier
Reads	100,000 per day	Unlimited
Writes	1,000 per day	Unlimited
Writes (same key)	1 per second	1 per second
Storage	1 GB	Unlimited
Key size	512 bytes	512 bytes
Value size	25 MiB	25 MiB
Metadata size	1024 bytes	1024 bytes

These are correct as of November 2023, and should be sufficient on the free tier for the majority of applications initially. You can see that KV is geared towards high-read applications with its limits, with the number of reads per day vastly higher than the number of writes on the free plan. When developing your applications in the future, keep these limits in mind.

That's it for this chapter; let's recap what's been covered.

What You've Learned

Although you didn't write much code, a lot was covered in this chapter in terms of caching using KV. You learned what caching is, and some of the use cases for using a cache. You created KV namespaces, and configured a Next.js

---

1.   https://developers.cloudflare.com/kv/platform/limits/

application to use that KV namespace using bindings. You then learned how to retrieve and store data from KV, as well as how to expire data in KV automatically. Finally, you learned how to see the data held in KV locally and on Cloudflare's servers, as well as how to see logs both locally and on Cloudflare's servers.

The full code for this project is available on GitHub.[2]

This is the last chapter where you'll work on the weather application. The next application you'll build will be able to handle image uploads, then use AI to analyze the uploaded images, and look at how you can introduce asynchronous capabilities into your applications using queues.

---

2.   https://github.com/apeacock1991/serverless-apps-on-cloudflare/tree/main/weather-app

## CHAPTER 9

Upload and Store Files on R2

Now let's see how we can upload and store objects. These objects, ranging from images to videos to PDFs, could be user uploaded or system generated.

Consider a video-sharing platform like YouTube, where users upload videos. Object storage, like AWS Simple Storage Service (S3), is ideal for securely storing such content. If you're familiar with AWS S3, you know that it involves creating buckets to store objects, with individual files having a max size of 5TB and no limits on objects or total bucket size.

Cloudflare provides a comparable product called R2, mirroring S3's core functionality. To make it easy to migrate from S3 to R2, Cloudflare has ensured the API for R2 is consistent with S3's API, effectively allowing you to switch from one to the other without any significant code changes.

In this chapter, you'll build a simple website enabling users to upload images. This single-page application (SPA) will be developed on Next.js. Upon image upload, a server-side route will handle storing the image on R2 and displaying it to the user.

Similar to previous applications, this one will evolve chapter by chapter. In the next chapter, Chapter 10, Analyze Images Using Workers AI, on page 129, you'll analyze image content using AI and render the results. In subsequent chapters (Chapter 11, Produce Messages to a Queue, on page 139, and Chapter 12, Consume Messages from a Queue, on page 151), you'll transition the application to be event-driven, using message queues for image processing.

Now, let's start the first iteration: uploading images to R2.

R2 Pricing

The significant advantage of R2 over S3 lies in its pricing. Unlike AWS, Cloudflare's R2 has no egress charges for data transfer to the internet. This departure from industry norms can lead to substantial cost savings. Take S3, for example, and you'll pay anywhere from $0.09 to $0.005 per GB for data transferred from S3 to the public internet.

Additionally, an infrequent access storage tier is currently in private beta. If you need to store data that is infrequently accessed, you can save money by marking it as infrequently accessed, or in the future, use lifecycle rules to automatically move data to that storage class that hasn't been accessed in a while.

R2 ensures the same 99.999999999 percent durability guarantee as S3, with an extremely low probability of losing an object within a vast object count—one object lost every 100,000 years for 1,000,000 stored objects, which is pretty crazy.

R2 is available on Cloudflare's free plan, allowing you to store up to 10GB, alongside 1 million Class A requests and 10 million Class B requests. Class A requests involve operations like listing buckets, writing to buckets, and copying objects, while Class B is mainly for reads. Beyond the free usage, a $5/month Workers Paid plan is required, with charges as follows: $0.015 per GB-month stored, $4.50 per million Class A requests, and $0.36 per million Class B requests.

Create a New Project

By now, I'm sure you know what the first step is when creating a new Cloudflare project. If you said:

```
$ npm create cloudflare@2.21.1 -- --no-auto-update
```

Then you were right! You can give it any name you like; I went for image-app.

For the options, they're the same as the last time:

- Select "website or web app," followed by "Next"
- Yes to TypeScript
- Don't use ESLint
- Don't use Tailwind CSS
- Use the src folder
- Use the app router

- Don't customize the default import aliases
- Don't deploy your application

Lastly, you can remove some of the files that have been created as you don't need them. Make sure you cd into image-app, then run:

```
$ rm -rf src/app/api/hello src/app/globals.css src/app/page.module.css
```

That's the bootstrapping complete; let's move on to building the application itself.

Create an R2 Bucket

Before you start writing code to handle image uploads, you'll need somewhere to store the images. As we covered at the start of the chapter, Cloudflare's object storage is called R2, and is perfect for handling your application's storage needs.

Similarly to other services you've used, you create an R2 bucket using Wrangler:

```
$ npx wrangler r2 bucket create <NAME>
```

You need to replace NAME with the name you want for your bucket. I went for image-app-uploads, so I ran:

```
$ npx wrangler r2 bucket create image-app-uploads
```

Accessing R2

 When running the command, you'll likely get a 10042 error code, asking you to enable R2. If you go to the Cloudflare dashboard, and click R2, you'll be guided to enter your card details. R2 is only available on the Workers Paid plan, which currently costs $5/month. At the time of writing, you won't be charged when you enter your card details though; you'll only be charged if your R2 usage goes beyond the free tier.

After a few seconds, you'll get confirmation that the bucket was created:

```
wrangler 3.53.1
-------------------
Creating bucket image-app-uploads with default storage class set to Standard.
Created bucket image-app-uploads with default storage class set to Standard.
```

A bucket is a basic organizational unit commonly used in object storage to group related objects together. Objects within a bucket represent individual pieces of data.

If you wanted to, there's nothing stopping you from storing completely unrelated things in the same bucket. However, my advice would be to always make sure your bucket has a single purpose in terms of the types of objects it stores.

In this case, the bucket will be responsible for storing all the files users upload. By default, the storage class is set to Standard. During Cloudflare's Developer Week 2024, they announced the ability to use different tiers for storage. Effectively, when the feature becomes generally available, you'll be able to reduce your costs for infrequently-accessed objects by around 90 percent.[1]

As resources that are bound to a Pages project are different for preview and production environments, you need to make a second bucket for preview environments:

```
$ npx wrangler r2 bucket create image-app-uploads-preview
```

With the bucket created, you need to make it available to your application, which you'll do next.

Data Migrations

If you already have a large amount of data on S3 and want to migrate it to R2, you have two options.

The first option is called Super Slurper, and, no, I'm not making that up, that's genuinely its name. It should be used for large, one-off migrations from S3 to R2. You effectively define a source bucket on S3, alongside an IAM policy, as well as a destination bucket on R2, and Cloudflare will migrate all of the data for you.

 The second option is called Sippy, another great name for a tool. Rather than being an all-at-once migration like Super Slurper, Sippy gradually migrates data from S3 to R2 as it's requested. Let's say you have a bucket on S3, with an object called "foo." When "foo" is requested, Cloudflare will retrieve it from S3 and store it in R2. And subsequent requests for that object will be served from R2, so you effectively gradually migrate data from S3 to R2 as and when it's requested.

You can find full details in Cloudflare's documentation.[2]

---

1.   https://blog.cloudflare.com/r2-events-gcs-migration-infrequent-access
2.   https://developers.cloudflare.com/r2/data-migration/

Bind an R2 Bucket

Similarly to how you exposed a KV namespace in Chapter 8, Cache Data with KV, on page 97, you need to do the same again here to expose the R2 bucket. Open the file, in the root of the project, named env.d.ts and add the following:

```
interface CloudflareEnv {
  IMAGE_APP_UPLOADS: R2Bucket;
}
```

With these modifications, your code is now aware that, at runtime, Cloudflare's environment should have access to an R2 bucket under the binding name IMAGE_APP_UPLOADS.

So that during local development your application can communicate with the R2 bucket, add the following configuration to the wrangler.toml file:

```
[[r2_buckets]]
binding = "IMAGE_APP_UPLOADS"
bucket_name = "image-app-uploads-preview"
```

In the last chapter, you used wrangler.toml to define any bindings. If you remember from that chapter, you defined different bindings for preview and production that you need to add too:

```
[[env.preview.r2_buckets]]
binding = "IMAGE_APP_UPLOADS"
bucket_name = "image-app-uploads-preview"

[[env.production.r2_buckets]]
binding = "IMAGE_APP_UPLOADS"
bucket_name = "image-app-uploads"
```

After the change, you should now have three sections defining R2 buckets. When a request is handled, Cloudflare will inject the correct binding based on the environment. For local development, it'll use the top-level r2_buckets bindings; for preview, it'll use env.preview.r2_buckets; and for production, it'll use env.production.r2_buckets.

With these adjustments, your R2 buckets are now bound to your new pages project. Let's make use of them.

Upload Files to R2

The first piece of the image application that you'll build will be the server-side route that handles file uploads. You already learned how to build a server-side route using Next.js in Chapter 7, Add a Back End to the Front End, on page 79, so I won't go into too much detail on the Next.js specifics in this chapter.

Create a new file at src/app/api/files/route.ts and add the following:

```
import { getRequestContext } from '@cloudflare/next-on-pages'

export const runtime = 'edge';

export async function POST(request: Request) {
  const bucket = getRequestContext().env.IMAGE_APP_UPLOADS;
  const body = await request.formData();
  const files = body.getAll('files');

  for(let x = 0; x < files.length; x++) {
    const f = files[x] as File;
    const uuid = crypto.randomUUID()

    await bucket.put(uuid, f)
  }
  return new Response('Images uploaded', {
    headers: { 'content-type': 'application/json' }
  });
}
```

The code is very simple, as this server-side route is effectively acting as a proxy to R2 currently. You'll be changing this route considerably as the application evolves. Let's walk through the code, starting with:

```
const bucket = getRequestContext().env.IMAGE_APP_UPLOADS;
const body = await request.formData();
const files = body.getAll('files');
```

As you've seen in prior chapters, you access any bindings in Cloudflare Pages projects by using getRequestContext().env.BINDING_NAME. Next, the form data is extracted from the request. As the application will handle file uploads, you can't use .json(), so the application will use form data instead. These are effectively key-value pairs, and as the name suggests, are most commonly used with forms.

When the user uploads files on the front end, they'll be passed to this server-side route under the files key. The user will be able to upload multiple files at once, so the second line retrieves all the files uploaded. With the files retrieved, the endpoint can now loop over each file:

```
for(let x = 0; x < files.length; x++) {
  const f = files[x] as File;
  const uuid = crypto.randomUUID()

  await bucket.put(uuid, f)
}
```

The first line retrieves the file to handle for this loop iteration, and casts it to a File as the compiler won't know what type it is otherwise.

On the second line, a Universally Unique Identifier (UUID) is generated, and on the third line, the image is stored in the R2 bucket.

As with all bindings, Cloudflare will always inject an object at runtime for you to use to access the resources provided by that binding. In this case, it will be an object that adheres to the interface defined by R2Bucket. That object will provide methods that allow you to interact with the R2 bucket.

To upload a file to R2, you make use of put, with the first parameter being the key, and the second being the value you want to store.

The key must be a string. The value can be any of the following:

- ReadableStream
- ArrayBuffer
- ArrayBufferView
- string
- null
- Blob

In this case, a file is asserted to be of type File using as File, which extends Blob.

For the key parameter, you could use the file name. However, a UUID is used to ensure that there are no collisions between different users uploading files of the same name.

The final line returns a success response from the endpoint, to indicate to the front end that the file was successfully uploaded.

The server-side endpoint is complete. When given a list of files, it'll upload them all to an R2 bucket.

Next, let's create the front end that will call this endpoint.

Create the Front End

To keep things simple, the application's front end will again be built using Bootstrap. In fact, it'll look remarkably similar in style to the weather application, just to avoid implementing two unique front ends.

To add Bootstrap to the application, run the following command:

```
npm install --save bootstrap prop-types
```

Once Bootstrap has installed, replace the current content in src/app/layout.tsx with:

```tsx
import 'bootstrap/dist/css/bootstrap.css';
import { Inter } from 'next/font/google'

const inter = Inter({ subsets: ['latin'] })

export const metadata = {
  title: 'AI Image Analyzer',
  description: 'Analyze any image.',
}

export default function RootLayout({
  children,
}: {
  children: React.ReactNode
}) {
  return (
    <html lang="en">
      <body className={inter.className}>
        {children}
      </body>
    </html>
  )
}
```

I won't go over the code, as it's pretty much identical to the base layout used in the weather application.

Next, you'll need to create the page that users will use to upload files. We'll cover the code in two parts, breaking it into the logic executed when a file is uploaded, and the UI that is rendered.

Let's first cover the logic that handles when a file is uploaded.

```tsx
'use client';

import React from "react";
import { ChangeEvent } from "react";
import { ImageList } from "@/components/ImageList";

export default function Home() {
  const handleChange = (event: ChangeEvent) => {
    const local_files = (event.target as HTMLInputElement).files;
    let localUploadedImages: Array<UserImage> = [];

    if (local_files == undefined || local_files.length === 0) {
      return;
    }
```

```
    let formData = new FormData();

    for (let x = 0; x < local_files.length; x++) {
      formData.append('files', local_files[x]);

      localUploadedImages.push(
        {
          url: URL.createObjectURL(local_files[x]),
          filename: local_files[x].name
        }
      )
    }
    const headers = {
      'content-type': "multipart/form-data"
    };

    fetch("/api/files", { body: formData, method: "post"})
      .then(response => {
        if (response.ok) {
          setUploadedImages(localUploadedImages);
        } else {
          // handle an error
        }
      })
  }
  const [uploadedImages, setUploadedImages] = React.useState(new Array());
```

The code starts by defining this as a client component, along with a few
required imports.

```
'use client';

import React from "react";
import { ChangeEvent } from "react";
import { ImageList } from "@/components/ImageList";
```

The last one is a yet-to-be-created component that you'll add shortly. It'll be
responsible for rendering the images that are uploaded.

Next, a Home function is defined that tells Next.js this is a page to render, and
you define your own function inside of that to handle when the user selects
images to be uploaded:

```
export default function Home() {

  const handleChange = (event: ChangeEvent) => {
    const local_files = (event.target as HTMLInputElement).files;
    let localUploadedImages: Array<UserImage> = [];

    if (local_files == undefined || local_files.length === 0) {
      return;
    }
```

When this function is triggered, it'll receive a change event, containing the target. In this case, it'll be an input field, containing any images the user selected, and those files are extracted at the top of the function.

You're going to store the uploaded images in an array, which is defined next. This array will contain objects of type UserImage, which you will define later.

Before making an API call to upload the images, you need to prepare the payload:

```
let formData = new FormData();

for (let x = 0; x < local_files.length; x++) {
  formData.append('files', local_files[x]);

  localUploadedImages.push(
    {
      url: URL.createObjectURL(local_files[x]),
      filename: local_files[x].name
    }
  )
}
```

As the server-side endpoint expects the payload as form data, the client-side code needs to prepare the request in that format. This is as simple as creating a new FormData object and calling append. When calling append, the first parameter is the name of the field, and the second parameter is the value.

You do this inside of a loop as there might be multiple files uploaded, and inside the same loop the file is pushed to the localUploadedImages array. Rather than retrieving the files from R2, you can render the images entirely on the client side without any network calls.

Lastly, you can make the call to the server-side endpoint:

```
const headers = {
  'content-type': "multipart/form-data"
};

fetch("/api/files", { body: formData, method: "post"})
  .then(response => {
    if (response.ok) {
      setUploadedImages(localUploadedImages);
    } else {
      // handle an error
    }
  })
}
const [uploadedImages, setUploadedImages] = React.useState(new Array());
```

When sending form data, you pass it in the body of the request, and typically use a POST request. Assuming the call is successful, some state is set that contains the uploaded images, with the state defined a little further down.

In the event the upload fails, you'll want to render an error message, but as there's already a fair amount of code for this page, I've left that out.

With the logic defined to handle the user selecting some images to upload, let's move on to rendering the UI.

```
  return (
    <section className="vh-100">
      <div className="container py-5 h-100">

        <div className="row d-flex justify-content-center align-items-center h-100">
          <div className="col-md-8 col-lg-6 col-xl-4">

            <h3 className="mb-4 pb-2 fw-normal"
                style={{textAlign: 'center'}}>
                AI Image Analyzer
            </h3>

            {uploadedImages.length === 0 && (
              <>
                <p>Select a number of images and upload
                  them to have them analyzed.</p>

                <div className="input-group rounded mb-3">
                  <input className="form-control rounded"
                         aria-label="Images"
                         type="file"
                         multiple onChange={handleChange}
                  />
                </div>
              </>
            )}

            {uploadedImages.length > 0 && (
              <>
                <p style={{textAlign: 'center'}}>
                  Files uploaded successfully.
                </p>

                <ImageList images={uploadedImages} />
              </>
            )}

          </div>
        </div>

      </div>
    </section>
  )
}
```

There's nothing particularly new here, as it's mostly just React. If there are no images stored in React's state, an input field is rendered so the user can upload some images. Once they select some images, and they've been successfully uploaded, those images are rendered using the ImageList component.

With the code explained, open src/app/page.tsx and replace the existing content with the two code blocks above.

As the code above references a custom interface to represent a user's uploaded image, that interface needs to be defined. Create a new file in the root of the project called additional.d.ts and add the following:

```
interface UserImage {
  filename: string;
  url: string;
}
```

Next.js will automatically load this file, or any other .d.ts files you wish to add, and any type definitions in those files.

Before testing the application, you need to create the ImageList component. In the same way it's good practice to segregate your back end code into separate parts, it's good practice to separate the front end components too.

Create a new file at src/components/ImageList/index.tsx and add the following:

```
import PropTypes from "prop-types";

type ImageListProps = {
  images: Array<UserImage>
}

export const ImageList = ({images}: ImageListProps) => {
  return (
    <div className="row d-flex justify-content-center align-items-center h-100">
      <div className="col-12">

      {Object.values(images).map((image, index) => {
        return (
          <>
            <div className="row d-flex">
              <div className="col-6">
                <img src={image.url}
                     width="100%" />
              </div>
              <div className="col-6">
                Image analysis will go here
              </div>
            </div>
            <hr />
          </>
```

```
        )
      })}

      </div>
    </div>
  )
}
ImageList.propTypes = {
  images: PropTypes.arrayOf(
    PropTypes.shape(
      {
        url: PropTypes.string.isRequired,
        filename: PropTypes.string.isRequired
      }
    )
  )
}
```

The component will be given an array of objects, with each object representing a file. Each file will contain a URL and a filename.

When the component is rendered, it iterates through each file that's passed to it, and displays a row for each one containing the uploaded image.

As the application isn't doing anything with the images yet, besides uploading them to an R2 bucket, the component renders some placeholder text for now. In Chapter 10, Analyze Images Using Workers AI, on page 129, the placeholder text will be replaced with the result of the analysis of the image.

That's all the code needed to allow users to upload images, and to store them in an R2 bucket. Let's test everything is working as expected.

Test R2 Uploads Locally

When you tested applications locally that made use of D1 and KV, Wrangler simulated those resources for you—it'll do the same for R2, as long as it exists in wrangler.toml and is defined in CloudflareEnv.

You can now run the application locally using npm run dev.

Once the application is running, press b to open the application in your browser, and try uploading an image. It should be pretty instantaneous as everything is happening locally.

You can verify the image was stored in the R2 bucket by checking the local .wrangler directory by running the following command:

```
$ ls -la .wrangler/state/v3/r2/
```

Each time you upload an image, you should see it stored in that folder. Note that the v3 part will change depending on Wrangler's major version, so if you end up using version 4 in the future, the path would have v4 in it. The folder name for the bucket may vary between operating systems.

If you retrieve a file from that folder and add the extension to it (e.g. .png) and open it, you'll see the image itself, just to prove it's been stored successfully.

With everything working locally, let's deploy the application to Cloudflare.

Deploy to Cloudflare

Deploying to Cloudflare is as simple as running npm run deploy.

After deployment, access the provided URL, and try uploading some images.

Since the application now runs on Cloudflare, it utilizes the previously created R2 buckets to store images. You can verify this is working as anticipated by using the Cloudflare dashboard.

Navigate to R2 in the left menu, and click on your bucket's name. If the deploy command was executed on the production branch, Cloudflare deploys to production; otherwise, it deploys to preview.

Once the page loads, you'll see a list of all the files in that bucket, as shown below.

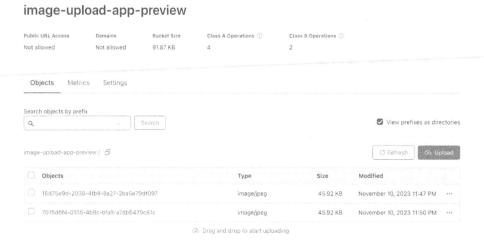

The UI will show you the type of each file, its size, as well as allow you to download or delete any file.

If you're not sure whether a deployment was made to preview or production, you can check in the Cloudflare dashboard by going to the project. Within the project, there'll be a list of deployments shown, each tagged with preview or production.

That's it for R2 buckets, and this completes another chapter. Let's recap what was covered.

What You've Learned

In this chapter, you learned to create R2 buckets to store objects that represent individual files. To get to grips with R2, you built a simple image uploader.

Now that users can upload images, in the next chapter, you'll learn how you can use one of Cloudflare's newest additions, AI, to analyze the images you upload.

## CHAPTER 10

Analyze Images Using Workers AI

Recently, one technology has exploded in popularity—Artificial Intelligence (AI). From conversing with ChatGPT to creating images with Stable Diffusion to writing code with the aid of GitHub Copilot, AI is everywhere.

Enter Cloudflare's 2023 launch of Workers AI, an AI offering with various models catering to diverse use cases. Whether text generation, language translation, or audio-to-text conversion, Cloudflare has a model for it.

Cloudflare's Workers AI seamlessly integrates into their platform, making it accessible from Workers and Pages. As of April 2024, it matured from a beta product to being generally available, and in this chapter, you'll have some fun using AI on Cloudflare's platform to classify uploaded images.

The application flow remains relatively unchanged in this chapter. The front end facilitates image uploads, and upon uploading, the back end analyzes the images while still uploading the file to R2. The analysis results are then returned to the front end for display.

Now that you understand what you are going to build in this chapter, let's get started.

Add an AI Binding

Adding a new binding to a Pages project is likely familiar by now. The distinction with AI is that there's no resource creation involved. You simply add the AI binding to gain complete access to Cloudflare's array of models.

To add a new AI binding to your project, open wrangler.toml and add the following:

```
[ai]
binding = "AI"

[env.preview.ai]
binding = "AI"

[env.production.ai]
binding = "AI"
```

There's no need to link to specific resources using IDs, as the models are all shared resources. If you have a keen eye, you might've noticed there's only a single bracket used, whereas other bindings use two brackets. This is due to TOML syntax, where single brackets define a table, and double brackets define an array. As there can only ever be one AI binding per environment, you use the table syntax for AI bindings, whereas for resources such as databases, you may need to bind multiple, so the array syntax is used.

Here are some of the models currently available:

- Text Generation: Llama 3, Mistral
- Speech recognition: OpenAI's Whisper
- Translation: M2M100
- Text Classification: Distilled BERT
- Image Classification: Resnet 50
- Image Generation: Stable Diffusion, Flux
- Text Embeddings: BAAI general embedding

All these AI models operate on Graphical Processing Units (GPUs), distinct from the Central Processing Units (CPUs) that execute your application code. GPUs, with their proficiency in handling enhanced mathematical computations, prove significantly more efficient for running AI models.

In order to support Workers AI, Cloudflare had to add GPUs to their global network. When it first launched, Cloudflare had seven locations with GPUs, which meant there was a fair amount of latency. However, at the time of writing, there are over 100 GPUs across Cloudflare's global network, with their aim to have GPUs running everywhere by the end of 2024.

With the AI binding configured, let's make the necessary code changes.

Execute AI Models

It blows my mind how easy it is to use AI these days. Just a couple of years ago, AI technologies felt like an alien concept; they were complex and required specialized training to use. Fast forward to 2024, and the rapid development of generative AI has democratized access to AI for everyone, regardless of their background.

For your application, you'll use the Resnet 50 model from Microsoft, an AI model designed for image classification. When presented with an image, the model provides a list of identified objects along with confidence scores. For instance, uploading an image of a cat should result in the model recognizing it as a cat, and in some cases, even specifying the breed.

Let's use some AI, by first updating the environment to expect the AI binding. Open env.d.ts and update CloudflareEnv to the following:

```
interface CloudflareEnv {
  IMAGE_APP_UPLOADS: R2Bucket;
  AI: any;
}
```

Cloudflare's documentation defines the type as any, so I've followed suit. I suspect in the future there'll be a defined type.

With the environment now expecting an AI binding to be injected at runtime, you can update the server-side endpoint defined at src/app/api/files/route.ts to the following:

```
import { getRequestContext } from '@cloudflare/next-on-pages'

export const runtime = 'edge';

export async function POST(request: Request) {
  const bucket = getRequestContext().env.IMAGE_APP_UPLOADS;
  const body = await request.formData();
  const files = body.getAll('files');
  const ai = getRequestContext().env.AI;
  let imageAnalysis = [];

  for(let x = 0; x < files.length; x++) {
    const f = files[x] as File;
    const uuid = crypto.randomUUID()

    await bucket.put(uuid, f);

    const blob = await f.arrayBuffer();

    const inputs = {
      image: Array.from(new Uint8Array(blob))
    };
```

```
    imageAnalysis.push(
      {
        id: uuid,
        name: f.name,
        analysis: await ai.run('@cf/microsoft/resnet-50', inputs)
      }
    )
  }
  return new Response(JSON.stringify({results: imageAnalysis}), {
    headers: { 'content-type': 'application/json' }
  });
}
```

Whenever you want to use bindings in Pages projects, you need to import getRequestContext to get access to them:

```
import { getRequestContext } from '@cloudflare/next-on-pages'
```

Then, to call a model, you use getRequestContext.env to access the environment where bindings will be set:

```
const ai = getRequestContext().env.AI;
let imageAnalysis = [];
```

You also need to create an empty array, which will be populated later in the function with the image analysis results that will be returned from the API. With the bindings retrieved, you can now call the model for each image uploaded:

```
const blob = await f.arrayBuffer();

const inputs = {
  image: Array.from(new Uint8Array(blob))
};

imageAnalysis.push(
  {
    id: uuid,
    name: f.name,
    analysis: await ai.run('@cf/microsoft/resnet-50', inputs)
  }
)
```

To call the Resnet 50 model, the image has to be converted to something a machine can understand. Therefore, you convert the image to a byte array using arrayBuffer, and then that is converted to an array of unsigned 8-bit integers, which is something the model can understand.

With the input prepared, the final line in this section calls the Resnet 50 model, pushing the results to the imageAnalysis array. When calling any AI model on Cloudflare, you always call the run method, with the first parameter being the model and the second being the input. If you're unsure how to format the input for a given model, Cloudflare has code examples.[1]

Lastly, the server-side endpoint returns the image analysis results:

```
return new Response(JSON.stringify({results: imageAnalysis}), {
  headers: { 'content-type': 'application/json' }
});
```

That's all that's required to call an AI model. Cloudflare has made it nearly effortless to use such a powerful tool.

Your work isn't done just yet though, as to see the model in action, you need to update the front end to render the image classification results.

Workers AI Limits

 As with most things, there are limits. At the time of writing, everyone gets 10,000 tokens free per day for text generation and embeddings, as well as 250 steps for images, and 10 minutes of audio. As Workers AI is available on the free plan, once you hit your daily limit, your requests will fail.

Cloudflare's documentation has a full list of limits by model.[2]

Render Image Classification Results

Similarly to the backend changes, the front end changes are relatively minimal too. With the server-side endpoint now returning the results of the image analysis done by the AI model, you just need to update the rendering logic to present them to the user.

As the API is now returning some additional data, you need some additional type definitions. Open additional.d.ts and update it like so:

```
interface UserImage {
  filename: string;
  url: string;
  analysis?: Array<Analysis>;
}

interface Analysis {
  label: string;
  score: number;
}
```

---

1. https://developers.cloudflare.com/workers-ai/models/
2. https://developers.cloudflare.com/workers-ai/platform/limits/

In the last iteration of the application, there was simply a filename and url. All that has been added is an optional analysis property, which contains an array of Analysis, which itself has a label and score. The analysis is an array because the model can return several guesses at what might be contained in the image.

The Resnet 50 model returns a list of possible labels, with a label representing what it thinks the image is, and a score, which is how confident it is in its analysis.

While we're on the topic of types, as you now have to do something with the parsed response, rather than just setting the files based on local data, you need to define a type to represent the response from the API endpoint. You can add this in additional.d.ts if you wish, but I prefer to define these sorts of types in the files they are used, at least if the API endpoint is only called from one location. Therefore, I added it to the top of src/app/page.tsx, before the Home function starts and after the imports:

```
type ImageUploadResult = {
  results: [
    {
      id: string,
      name: string,
      analysis: Array<Analysis>
    }
  ]
}
```

With the type definitions ready, you need to amend the fetch to /api/files to be the following, in the same src/app/page.tsx file:

```
fetch("/api/files", { body: formData, method: "post"})
  .then(response => response.json<ImageUploadResult>())
  .then(response => {
    for(let x = 0; x < response.results.length; x++) {
      let image = localUploadedImages.find(
        i => i.filename === response.results[x].name
      );

      if (image) {
        image.analysis = response.results[x].analysis;
      }
    }
  })
  .then(response => {
    setUploadedImages(localUploadedImages);
  })
```

Rather than immediately setting the state to the uploaded images, you now need to iterate through the results returned, and if an analysis has been returned for a given image, update that image's analysis property. To do this, you first need to find the image based on the filename, and if one is found, update it accordingly.

Once all the results have been iterated through, each image should have its analysis associated with it, so you can set the React state to contain the list of images along with their analysis.

Now that the React state is being updated with the image analysis results, the final change is in src/components/ImageList/index.tsx to render the analysis on the page. Find the section that was hard-coded to show that image analysis was to be added:

```
<div className="col-6">
    Image analysis will go here
</div>
```

And replace it with the following:

```
{image.analysis && (
    <div className="col-6">
        { image.analysis.map((a) => (<>{a.label}: {a.score}<br /><br /></>)) }
    </div>
)}
{!image.analysis && (
    <div className="col-6">
        Image analysis is pending
    </div>
)}
```

The component now has two states for the analysis section. The first is used when image analysis results are available, and it simply iterates over the analysis and renders them one after the other. The second state is when the analysis is pending, which will be shown while the images are uploaded and the model is executed on the back end.

With all those changes made, let's analyze some images with AI.

Test Applications that Use AI

Similarly to the previous chapters, you have the ability to test your application locally using Wrangler before deploying it to Cloudflare's network, even when using AI models. As discussed in the introduction, these models are often large and demand substantial memory to run, so they won't run on your local machine. Instead, it'll make a remote call to Cloudflare's network and it'll accrue usage charges. To test locally, start the application using npm run dev.

Cloudflare API

Throughout the book, you've used Wrangler or the dashboard to create and bind resources. This is by far the most used approach, but Cloudflare does provide a large API that you can alternatively use.

For example, you can execute an AI model via API instead.[y] In short, you issue a POST request to https://api.cloudflare.com/client/v4/accounts/{account_identifier}/ai/run/{model_name} and it'll return the response from the model.

Along the same lines, you can create a D1 database using https://api.cloudflare.com/client/v4/accounts/{account_identifier}/d1/database and query it using the API.[z]

A full list of endpoints are available in Cloudflare's API documentation.[aa]

Once you've tested locally, you can deploy your project by executing `npm run deploy` in the project's root. After deployment, visit the URL provided in the terminal, upload a few images, and observe the AI model's predictions for the image content. The scores, ranging from 0 to 1, signify the model's confidence in the assigned labels. The closer the score is to 1, the more certain the model is of that label. The screenshot is an example of what you might observe after uploading images.

I'd recommend testing with file sizes that aren't too large, and stick to common image formats like JPG and PNG, as I've found the most success with those. It may take a few seconds after selecting an image for anything to update in the UI, while it waits for the AI model to execute.

That's the end of this chapter; let's recap what we covered.

Files uploaded successfully.

SAMOYED:
0.33282172679901123

GREAT PYRENEES:
0.21372255682945251

KUVASZ:
0.17130544781684875

SIBERIAN HUSKY:
0.06164443865418434

SIAMESE CAT:
0.04306143894791603

PICKET FENCE:
0.2507365345954895

BOATHOUSE:
0.24226272106170654

CHURCH:
0.2193894237279892

BEACON:
0.07574689388275146

BARN:
0.0332208563923835754

AI Gateway and Vectorize

Although not covered in this book, Cloudflare has other AI products that you may want to use. The first is AI Gateway, which is essentially a special kind of API gateway but specifically for AI.

Rather than routing requests directly to model providers such as OpenAI, Anthropic, Bedrock or HuggingFace, you can send them through Cloudflare's AI gateway free of charge (some features in the future might incur additional costs). Cloudflare will then give you insights into the information sent such as token counts and response times, allow you to cache data to save money on repeat requests, evaluate a model's performance, and even retry/fallback mechanisms.

The second product is called Vectorize, Cloudflare's globally distributed vector database. If you've ever added Retrieval Augmented Generation to an application, the chances are you used a vector database. In short, it allows you to store representations of text or images as vectors, and then query those vectors. For example, you could use it for semantic search for an e-commerce website that lists a lot of products, allowing you to find the most relevant products based on a user's search query.

What You've Learned

In this chapter, you learned about the AI models Cloudflare has to offer, and how to execute them from a Pages project.

You may have noticed that so far, you haven't used the images that are being uploaded to the R2 bucket you created in the last chapter. In the next chapter, you'll use that R2 bucket, as you significantly change how the application functions, by exploring how you can build asynchronous applications, and complete asynchronous tasks, using a queue.

If you want to see how the project looks code-wise before you significantly change it, you can do so on GitHub.[6]

---

6.   https://github.com/apeacock1991/serverless-apps-on-cloudflare/tree/main/image-app

## CHAPTER 11

Produce Messages to a Queue

Throughout the book, we've focused on applications interacting through synchronous communication. For instance, in Chapter 7, Add a Back End to the Front End, on page 79, the server-side route was directly called from the front end. Even though the front end code used Promises, which are asynchronous, the interaction itself remained synchronous, involving point-to-point communication.

Synchronous communication is appropriate when you need whatever data is being served from the back end right away. In the weather application, users expect to see the weather without delay.

Now consider an e-commerce scenario where a user makes a purchase. The final step involves payment processing, usually done synchronously for immediate issue resolution. The system may also generate an invoice email with a PDF attachment. It might make sense to send the email with the PDF attached asynchronously, as it's not critical to the immediate workflow. Although it needs to occur eventually, a slight delay in receiving the invoice wouldn't impact the critical path of the payment process.

When introducing new features to an application, one of the most common questions you might ask is: can this be handled asynchronously? If it can, maybe it should be.

We'll cover the basics of asynchronous architecture throughout this chapter. For a deeper understanding, I recommend reading *Fundamentals of Software Architecture* by Neal Ford and Mark Richards.

In the upcoming two chapters, you'll enhance the image analysis application. While there won't be any changes in functionality, there'll be a significant shift in the application's architecture.

Currently, when images are uploaded, the application uploads them to an R2 bucket, analyzes them with AI, and returns the analysis to the user. You'll migrate the image analysis to occur as part of an asynchronous workflow, detached from the HTTP request triggered during image uploads. In this chapter, you'll produce messages to the queue, and in the next chapter, you'll consume messages from the queue and analyze the queued images.

To facilitate the asynchronous workflow, you'll leverage another Cloudflare product called Queues. This tool allows you to create queues, add message data to a queue, and have a separate Worker consume messages from the queue.

Queues are part of the $5/month Workers Paid plan and are not accessible on the free plan.

During the HTTP request to upload images, you'll add a message to the queue and promptly return a response to the front end. This ensures quick processing of the HTTP request, as adding a message to a queue is a quick operation. After the HTTP request concludes, the front end can then poll a separate endpoint to retrieve the image analysis results.

The flow can be broken down into a few sequence diagrams to help visualize all the pieces of the puzzle. Here are the steps needed to upload an image, and publish a message in the queue for analysis:

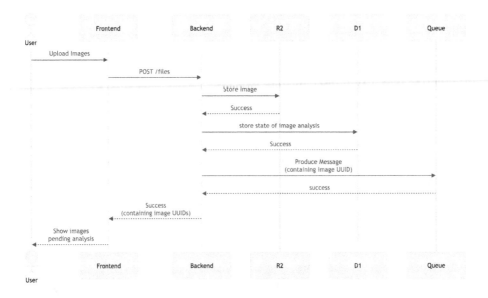

In summary, the images will be uploaded to R2, and an initial row will be inserted into a D1 database per image to track the status of the image analysis. In Chapter 12, Consume Messages from a Queue, on page 151, the status of the image analysis will be updated in the D1 database once the image analysis has been completed. Finally, a message is produced to the queue. Once that happens, the front end can poll a separate endpoint for the status of the results, and the consumer can process any images in the queue for analysis:

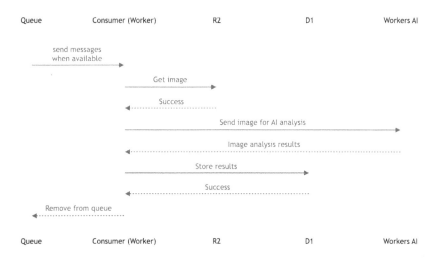

This part of the flow will be implemented in the next chapter, but I think it's important for you to understand the end-to-end flow, and where you're eventually heading.

It may look quite complicated, and it's definitely more complex than the architecture you had before, but as discussed, there are several upsides to this approach. In this particular example, let's say you allow users to upload up to fifty images, and it takes three seconds to analyze each image—that's two and a half minutes.

The user would have to wait the whole duration before seeing any results, and what happens if there's an error processing one of the images? Does the entire request fail? Do you retry that one image, resulting in even longer processing times? What happens if you start hitting limits on the AI models? What if the user's connection drops for a brief second, and as a result the HTTP request fails?

These problems are largely alleviated by using a queue. The user will see gradual results being displayed, if there's an error they won't see the results for that one image, or you can easily retry that failed image again in the background. If you're hitting request limits, you can tune the amount of concurrent workers that are able to handle messages so that you stay within the limits.

I find building these types of applications incredibly fun and rewarding, so I hope you do too. Let's get started.

Add a Queue

The first task you will need to complete is to add a new queue. You might've come across queues before, perhaps using a popular framework such as RabbitMQ, or perhaps in a Ruby environment with Sidekiq, or even on AWS using their Simple Queueing Service (SQS).

If you have, you'll likely be familiar with exactly how they work. If not, I'll explain them at a high level as you progress through the chapter.

To add a new queue, you'll need to run the following command:

```
$ npx wrangler queues create <name>
```

The only parameter you need to provide is the name, so for this project I named it image-analysis, and ran the following two commands:

```
$ npx wrangler queues create image-analysis
$ npx wrangler queues create image-analysis-preview
```

Similarly to other chapters, the application needs to create two resources: one to use for the main production branch, and one to use for all preview branches.

After a few seconds, you'll receive confirmation that the queues have been created.

When you come to update the application's code, the current server-side endpoint will add a message to the queue, and a separate Worker will be responsible for consuming from the queue, where the image analysis will happen. The state of the image analysis will be held in a database, with the front end polling a new server-side endpoint to see if the image analysis is available yet.

As you will need a D1 database too, let's quickly create that as well:

```
npx wrangler d1 create image-analysis
npx wrangler d1 create image-analysis-preview
```

Make sure to take note of the two database_id's returned from the create commands, as you'll need this later on.

With the queues and databases created, you can bind them to the project. As you've done before, you need to do this in wrangler.toml:

```
# Local
[[d1_databases]]
binding = "DB" # i.e. available in your Worker on env.DB
database_name = "image-analysis-preview"
database_id = "ec99f664-bfde-4126-95e8-105b8dd196c4"

[[queues.producers]]
queue = "image-analysis-preview"
binding = "ANALYSIS_QUEUE"

# Preview
[[env.preview.d1_databases]]
binding = "DB" # i.e. available in your Worker on env.DB
database_name = "image-analysis-preview"
database_id = "ec99f664-bfde-4126-95e8-105b8dd196c4"

[[env.preview.queues.producers]]
queue = "image-analysis-preview"
binding = "ANALYSIS_QUEUE"

# Production
[[env.production.d1_databases]]
binding = "DB" # i.e. available in your Worker on env.DB
database_name = "image-analysis"
database_id = "53d7c187-7398-4e17-8553-eaa1b0d7fc34"

[[env.production.queues.producers]]
queue = "image-analysis"
binding = "ANALYSIS_QUEUE"
```

You'll need to update database_id fields to be the IDs returned when you run the create command in Add a Queue, on page 142. Make sure to use the preview IDs for local and preview, and production for production. As the AI analysis will now happen in the consumer, you can remove the AI bindings from wrangler.toml too.

Now that your Pages project has all its bindings set up, let's update the current code to publish to the queue.

Publish to a Queue

Before you dive into updating the code, let's briefly go over the changes that are needed. Currently, when an image is uploaded, it's stored in an R2 bucket, and then analyzed in the server-side route.

Once you're finished with the code changes to the server-side route, it'll complete the following steps for each image:

1. Generate a UUID for the image
2. Store the image in R2
3. Insert a row into a D1 database to store the state of the image analysis
4. Publish a message to the image analysis queue

Once all the images have gone through each of these steps, the endpoint returns all the UUIDs for the images to the front end. The front end can then use those UUIDs to poll the state of the images that's stored in D1, once you add the endpoint to poll for results later.

To start, let's update Cloudflare's environment to expect the Queue binding. Open env.d.ts, and add in the new binding:

```
interface CloudflareEnv {
  IMAGE_APP_UPLOADS: R2Bucket;
  ANALYSIS_QUEUE: Queue;
  DB: D1Database;
}
```

You'll probably notice that the AI binding has been removed, which is intentional as the AI model will be called from another project when you add the consumer.

As with all the other bindings, the correct binding for the environment will be injected at runtime, and you'll be provided a simple client to interact with the resource that's bound. In this case, it will be an object that implements the Queue interface, for which you can see available methods in Cloudflare's documentation.[1]

With the binding now available to the application, open src/app/api/files/route.ts and replace the current server-side route with the following:

```
import uploadImageForAnalysis from "@/lib/upload_image_for_analysis";

export const runtime = 'edge';

interface ImageForAnalysis {
  filename: string;
  id: string;
}

export async function POST(request: Request) {
  const body = await request.formData();
  const files = body.getAll('files');
  let user_images = new Array<ImageForAnalysis>();
```

---

1. https://developers.cloudflare.com/queues/platform/javascript-apis/#producer

```
  for(let x = 0; x < files.length; x++) {
    const file = files[x] as File;
    const uuid = await uploadImageForAnalysis(file);

    user_images.push(
      {
        filename: file.name,
        id: uuid
      }
    )
  }

  return new Response(JSON.stringify(user_images), {
    headers: { 'content-type': 'application/json' }
  });
}
```

I'm a firm believer in writing readable code, so rather than keep adding to the server-side route itself, the primary logic of the route is extracted to a separate function, aptly named uploadImageForAnalysis.

The rest of the file is largely the same, with the exception of the response. As the image analysis will no longer happen in this route, the response no longer returns any analysis, and instead just returns the filename and its UUID.

With the server-side route updated, you need to implement the uploadImageFor-Analysis function. I chose to add it to the lib directory, as I prefer to keep the app-specific stuff in that folder, but you can place it wherever, as long as the import correctly references that function. Create a new file at src/lib/upload_image_for_analysis.ts and insert the following code:

```
import { getRequestContext } from '@cloudflare/next-on-pages';

const uploadImageForAnalysis = async(file: File): Promise<string> => {
  const uuid = crypto.randomUUID();
  const bucket = getRequestContext().env.IMAGE_APP_UPLOADS;
  const db = getRequestContext().env.DB;
  const queue = getRequestContext().env.ANALYSIS_QUEUE;

  await bucket.put(uuid, file);

  await db
        .prepare('INSERT INTO images (id, completed) VALUES (?1, 0)')
        .bind(uuid)
        .run()

  await queue.send(uuid);
  return uuid;
}

export default uploadImageForAnalysis;
```

This function is implementing the steps outlined in Publish to a Queue, on page 143. The first two lines have simply been moved from the server-side route, but the last two are worth going over:

```
await db
    .prepare('INSERT INTO images (id, completed) VALUES (?1, 0)')
    .bind(uuid)
    .run()
```

This should look familiar from Chapter 4, Persist Data with D1, on page 33, but to recap, this line is inserting a new record into a table called images. This is the table that will hold the current state of any images that are uploaded and their associated analysis.

The function inserts a new row containing the UUID of the image, and sets the completed field to 0, to indicate the analysis hasn't been completed yet. There are two more columns in the table: analysis and created_at, which are defaulted to NULL and the current time, respectively. You'll create the table shortly, via a migration.

When the image analysis is completed by the Worker that will consume from the queue, it will update its associated database row with the image analysis, and mark the row as completed. You could argue the completed column is obsolete, but I like the explicitness of it.

The other new line publishes a new message to the queue:

```
await queue.send(uuid);
```

As with all the client objects Cloudflare injects for you, I find it to be incredibly simple and intuitive. As you need to add a message to the queue, you simply call send and pass the contents of the message, often referred to as the body.

You can put a large number of data types in the body, as long as the object can be cloned. You can see all of the supported types in Mozilla's documentation, but all the main ones you'd expect are supported: String, Number, Array, and (plain) Object, to name a few.[2]

In this case, the UUID of the image is added to the queue, which is a string.

Before testing that messages are being produced to the Queue, you need to create the table needed to hold the state of the image analysis. As this has been covered extensively before, I'll zip through the changes needed. First, you need to create a new migration:

---

2.   https://developer.mozilla.org/en-US/docs/Web/API/Web_Workers_API/Structured_clone_algorithm#supported_types

```
$ npx wrangler d1 migrations \
    create image-analysis-preview create-image-analysis-table
```

That will create a new file under the migrations folder, likely named 0001_create-image-analysis-table.sql. Open that file, and append the following:

```
CREATE TABLE images (
  id TEXT PRIMARY KEY,
  analysis TEXT,
  completed INTEGER,
  created_at TEXT DEFAULT CURRENT_TIMESTAMP
);
```

Lastly, you need to actually execute the migration so that the table exists. You'll need to run it three times: once for local, once for the preview database, and once for the production database. The first two are the easiest, and can be achieved by running the following two commands:

```
$ npx wrangler d1 migrations apply image-analysis-preview --local
$ npx wrangler d1 migrations apply image-analysis-preview --remote
```

This is admittedly a little fiddly, and hopefully in future, Cloudflare can find a better way, but for now to execute migrations against production, you need to update wrangler.toml again. Update database_name to be image-analysis, and update the database_id to be the ID for your non-preview database in the top-level [[d1_databases]] section.

Once the changes are saved, you can run the last migration for production:

```
$ npx wrangler d1 migrations apply image-analysis --remote
```

Once the migration has finished, switch the configuration back to the preview databases, just to ensure you don't accidentally push data to your production database from your local testing.

Generally, I wouldn't recommend deploying schema changes to production from your device anyway in the long term. While you're learning the platform, it's a quick and easy way to get started, but in Chapter 14, Automate Workers & Pages Deployments, on page 193, we'll cover how to deploy schema changes as part of deployments, which is a far safer and more sustainable approach.

Those are all the changes you need in order to send to a queue, as well as to store state that can be shared between your producer and consumer. Although there's no consumer yet, you can still test that messages are being produced successfully.

View Messages on the Dashboard

After modifying the server-side route handling file uploads, the route now publishes a message to the image analysis queue.

Even though there is no consumer yet, and the front end hasn't been updated based on the new server-side code and its updated response, you can still verify that messages are being published to the queue.

Before that though, you need to deploy the updated code to Cloudflare. To do so, run `npm run deploy` and wait for it to finish. You can run queues locally too, but I find it's easier to use the dashboard on Cloudflare's servers. Furthermore, in the next chapter, it won't be possible to see an end-to-end flow locally, so we might as well start using Cloudflare's servers now.

Once the deployment is complete, open the URL output in the terminal, and upload an image as done previously. Currently, the front end won't function correctly, will likely produce errors and not show any change when you upload files. This is expected since the front end code hasn't been updated to accommodate the new flow. However, if you inspect the Developer Tools, you'll notice the server-side route returned a 200 OK response, indicating success.

Navigate to the Cloudflare dashboard, and under Workers & Pages, you'll find a subheading named Queues. Click on it to see a list of Queues associated with your account. Since you created a queue for preview and a queue for production, one will be marked as inactive, indicating no messages are being produced or consumed, while the other will be active, indicating messages are flowing to that queue.

The active queue will depend on whether you deployed to preview or production, which is determined by the local branch you are using. To make things easy for the next chapter, I would recommend making sure your application is deployed to the production environment.

Click on the active queue, and you'll be presented with metrics displaying the number of produced and consumed messages, along with retries and backlog. We'll dig into the meanings of these metrics when implementing the consumer.

At the top of the page, you'll find a small submenu containing Metrics, Messages, and Settings. Click on Messages, followed by the List Messages button. Leave the batch size as 10 and hit List Messages again. After a few seconds, you'll see a screen that looks like this:

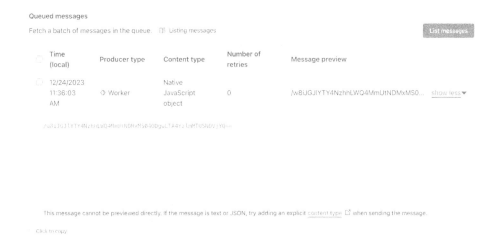

The batch size on the previous screen will determine how many messages are displayed, so if you've uploaded more than ten test images, only ten will be visible.

As shown in my example, there's one message in the queue. You can see when it was produced to the queue, its content type, the number of times the message has been retried, and the content of that message.

By default, messages are produced with a content type of json. As the application sends a string, you can set the content type when producing a message. To do so, open src/lib/upload_image_for_analysis.ts and update the line that sends the message to the queue:

```
await process.env.ANALYSIS_QUEUE.send(uuid, { contentType: "text" });
```

The send method has an optional second parameter to provide a list of options, with the only option currently supported being the content type. There are four possible values for the content type:

- json (default)
- text
- bytes
- v8

The v8 option represents a JavaScript object, which must be able to be cloned. You can use bytes to send an ArrayBuffer, which you could have used to send the image in binary format. The contents of both of these types will not be viewable in the dashboard.

The other two behave as you might expect: text allows you to send a string, and json allows you to send JSON. Both of these are viewable in the dashboard.

With the change made, redeploy your application using npm run deploy, access the new URL for that deployment from the terminal, and try uploading another image. Follow the steps to view messages on the dashboard again, and for the new message, you should see its content type updated.

While you can't do anything with the messages on the dashboard, you can at least see that messages are being successfully produced. If they are in a readable format such as text or JSON, you can additionally see that the messages are in the format you expect.

R2 Event Notifications

 If you've ever used S3, you may have seen you can trigger a Lambda function when an object is uploaded to a bucket. You can do the exact same with R2, using what Cloudflare calls Event Notifications. However, rather than invoking a Worker directly, a message will be published to a queue of your choosing, where a Worker can then consume that message—something you're about to learn all about.

What You've Learned

In this chapter, you learned or reviewed the key concepts around asynchronous workflows, and you implemented an asynchronous workflow using Queues on Cloudflare, and you learned how to produce messages to that queue. You verified that messages were being produced to the queue using the Cloudflare dashboard.

To handle messages produced to the queue, you need to create and assign a consumer to that queue, which is what you'll tackle in the next chapter.

## CHAPTER 12

Consume Messages from a Queue

In the previous chapter, you enhanced the image analysis application to produce messages to a queue whenever an image was uploaded. You now have messages sitting in a queue waiting to be processed. To handle the processing of these messages, you'll add a consumer in this chapter.

Different technologies that involve consuming messages have various methods to handle this. For example, Kafka requires running a consumer that pulls messages from a specified topic (similar to a queue). In contrast, Cloudflare simplifies the process significantly, treating a consumer as just another Worker, with minimal heavy lifting for engineers.

In the same way you built an API with a Worker in Chapter 1, Deploy Your First Cloudflare Worker, on page 1, you need to follow similar steps to allow a Worker to consume messages from a queue.

When adding the authentication Worker in Chapter 5, Worker-to-Worker Communication, on page 53, you created the Worker completely separate to the rest of the code, and they lived separately under version control in different repositories. I advocate keeping things that commonly change at the same time together, so when adding the consumer, we'll go for another approach: including both the full-stack application and the consumer in the same folder. If they were committed to version control, they would appear as individual folders within the same repository.

To achieve this, you first need to move the existing code for the front end into its own folder within the image application folder. Make sure you're one level above the image-app folder (or whatever you named your folder), and execute the following commands:

```
$ mkdir image-app/frontend && mv -f image-app/{.,}* image-app/frontend/
$ mv image-app/frontend/.git image-app/.git
```

This will create a new folder named frontend in the image-app folder, and move all the existing contents to that folder. If you prefer, you can make this change yourself using your operating system's UI.

With the front end moved to its own folder, make sure you're in the image-app folder (but not the frontend folder) once more and run create Cloudflare once again:

```
$ npm create cloudflare@2.21.1 -- --no-auto-update
```

For the name, enter image-analysis-consumer to reflect its purpose. For the rest of the prompts, select the following:

- For the type, select Queue consumer & producer Worker

- Elect to use TypeScript

- Do not use Git, as you're effectively adding this to an existing Git repository

- Don't deploy

Once the create command completes, you can navigate into the newly-created project (cd image-analysis-consumer) and you'll see a bunch of files has been created.

At a glance, you might struggle to see the differences between what's been created for this Worker that's going to consume messages, and one that's responding to HTTP requests. That's because there are very few differences, and enabling a Worker to consume from a queue is really simple.

To understand how a Worker can consume messages, let's first take a look at the src/index.ts file:

```
export interface Env {
        MY_QUEUE: Queue;
}

export default {
  async fetch(
    req: Request,
    env: Env,
    ctx: ExecutionContext
  ): Promise<Response> {
    await env.MY_QUEUE.send({
      url: req.url,
      method: req.method,
      headers: Object.fromEntries(req.headers),
    });

    return new Response('Sent message to the queue');
  },
```

```
  async queue(batch: MessageBatch<any>, env: Env): Promise<void> {
    for (let message of batch.messages) {
      console.log("Message received");
    }
        },
};
```

The Worker created with the create Cloudflare command is designed to both produce and consume messages from a queue. In the fetch function, which responds to HTTP requests, a message is produced to a queue, similar to what the image application already does.

For a Worker to consume messages, you need to define a queue function, which is called whenever messages are published to the queue. This function takes two parameters: a list of messages and the environment, containing secrets and bindings.

You're already familiar with how the environment works, but you might wonder why there's a batch of messages sent, not a single message. It's about efficiency. If your consumer has high throughput, processing messages in batches reduces the time spent retrieving messages from the queue, which involves network operations.

Later in this chapter, we'll explore how you can adjust the number of messages sent in a batch, as well as how Cloudflare determines when to send a batch of messages to a consumer.

You can also provide a type for the message body of each message in the batch. In the example above, where there is MessageBatch<any>, you can replace any with a more explicit type. For instance, use a string if you're dealing with a simple string, or JSON, or perhaps ArrayBuffer if you're sending messages in that format.

The logic you want to execute when a message is published goes into the queue function, where you must iterate over each message in the batch. Even if a single message is waiting to be processed, it'll still be passed as a batch.

Here's the interface for MessageBatch:

```
interface MessageBatch<Body = unknown> {
  readonly queue: string;
  readonly messages: Message<Body>[];
  ackAll(): void;
  retryAll(): void;
}
```

It's pretty lightweight, providing you with the name of the queue, and a list of messages. You can assign multiple queues to a single Worker, so if you need to tell what queue a message came from, you can use the queue property.

There are two methods too, ackAll and retryAll. Before a message is removed from the queue, it needs to be acknowledged as processed. We'll get into the different ways you can acknowledge messages later in the chapter, but for now, ackAll would acknowledge all the messages as processed, and retryAll would re-queue the entire batch.

The other file of interest is the wrangler.toml, which looks like this:

```
name = "image-analysis-consumer"
main = "src/index.ts"
compatibility_date = "2023-12-18"

[[queues.producers]]
binding = "MY_QUEUE"
queue = "my-queue"

[[queues.consumers]]
queue = "my-queue"
# max_batch_size = 10
# max_batch_timeout = 30
# max_retries = 10
# dead_letter_queue = "my-queue-dlq"
```

As this is a Worker, you use this file to inform Cloudflare that this Worker intends to consume from a specific queue. If you want to allow a Worker to produce messages to a queue, you achieve that using a binding too. Simply provide the name you want to use in your code for the binding and the name of the queue, and you'll be able to produce to that queue.

In this project, the Worker will only be responsible for consuming and will have no need to produce. However, it's useful to understand how to configure Workers to produce messages.

To configure a Worker to consume from a queue, you specify the name of the queue you want to consume from, and that's the only required information. The other configuration options, currently commented out, all have sensible defaults, but you can adjust them if needed. Here's what each one means:

- max_batch_size defines the maximum number of messages that each batch can contain. It defaults to 10, meaning that when the queue function is called, there will be at most 10 messages to process. However, there might be fewer, which is where the next configuration comes into play.

- max_batch_timeout sets the maximum amount of time, in seconds, to wait for a batch to be full. The default is set to 5, which means that as soon as a message is in the queue, Cloudflare will wait at most 5 seconds until it delivers messages. Messages will be delivered either when a batch is full (based on max_batch_size) or when the max_batch_timeout is reached. This ensures that messages never wait too long to be handled, and you can adjust it as needed.

- max_retries determines how many times each message is processed before it goes into the dead letter queue (DLQ). If a message fails to be processed, it'll be retried until the number of attempts exceeds max_retries. By default, if any message in a batch fails to be processed, all messages in that batch will be marked as failed and retried. The default value is set to 3.

- dead_letter_queue allows you to define a queue where messages are placed if a message is attempted to be processed more than max_retries. If a message fails to be processed and retried the specified number of times, it'll be placed in the dead letter queue. You can assign a Worker to consume from the dead letter queue and handle failed messages. If you don't define a dead letter queue, messages that are retried and exceed max_retries are discarded from the queue. If you define a dead letter queue but don't define a consumer for that queue, messages will be deleted from the dead letter queue after four days.

- max_concurrency is not in the provided configuration but is available for use. In a serverless environment, an invocation of your Worker acting as a consumer will be created to handle batches. Cloudflare will automatically create more invocations of your Worker to handle demand, based on the size of the queue. If the number of messages in the queue increases faster than the current number of invocations can consume messages, Cloudflare will create more invocations, up until the maximum allowed (250). If your consumer is regularly retrying messages, it may prevent your consumer from scaling up to meet demand. By default, this setting is set to the maximum (250). However, you may need to limit the number of concurrent invocations due to downstream limits, such as API limits for a service your consumer interacts with. If that's the case, it's better to lower max_concurrency to a point where you're under those limits rather than letting the consumer fail and retry, which will eventually scale your invocations down to 1, significantly reducing your throughput.

For now, Cloudflare sets sensible defaults for everything, and I'd only change these settings if and when you need to, based on usage and how the application performs when deployed. In terms of throughput, each queue can process five thousand messages per second.

Armed with this knowledge, let's update these two files to handle the use case for the image application: analyzing the images in the queue with AI.

First, open wrangler.toml and update it to the following:

```
name = "image-analysis-consumer"
main = "src/index.ts"
compatibility_date = "2023-12-18"

[[queues.consumers]]
queue = "image-analysis"

[ai]
binding = "AI"

[[d1_databases]]
binding = "DB"
database_name = "image-analysis"
database_id = "xxx"

[[r2_buckets]]
binding = 'IMAGE_APP_UPLOADS'
bucket_name = 'image-app-uploads'
```

There's not too much new here, as you've created several bindings before. Effectively, as the processing is no longer happening in the Pages project, the majority of the bindings are present in the consumer instead. The Pages project still needs access to the D1 database, and the R2 bucket, but the rest of the bindings can be removed from the Pages project via the dashboard. Make sure you update the database_id for the D1 database to reflect the ID of your production database.

You may notice there's no mention of preview bindings here, so you'll need to make sure you're doing everything on the main/master branch, so that it's deployed to production. To keep things simple, we're just going to make use of production, and we'll cover environments for Workers in Chapter 15, Deploy to Production, on page 213. If you did use preview in the last chapter—no worries, just make sure you use preview resources here too.

Let's create the consumer. Replace the contents of src/index.ts with the following:

```
export interface Env {
        IMAGE_APP_UPLOADS: R2Bucket;
        DB: D1Database;
        ANALYSIS_QUEUE: Queue;
```

```
        AI: any;
}
export default {
  async queue(batch: MessageBatch<string>, env: Env): Promise<void> {
    for (let message of batch.messages) {
      const image_id = message.body
      const image = await env.IMAGE_APP_UPLOADS.get(image_id);

      if (image === null) {
        console.log(`Could not find image ID ${image_id}`);

        message.retry();
        continue;
      }

      const inputs = {
        image: Array.from(
          new Uint8Array(await image.arrayBuffer())
        )
      };

      const analysis = await env.AI.run('@cf/microsoft/resnet-50', inputs);

      await env.DB
        .prepare(
          'UPDATE images SET completed = 1, analysis = ?1 WHERE id = ?2'
        )
        .bind(JSON.stringify(analysis), image_id)
        .run();

      await env.IMAGE_APP_UPLOADS.delete(image_id);

      message.ack();
    }
  },
};
```

For the most part, this code should look largely familiar. The majority of it has been migrated from the Pages project to the consumer. The fetch function has been removed, as this Worker has no need to respond to HTTP requests, and you're left with the queue function.

Just to ensure everything makes sense, let's step through section by section.

```
async queue(batch: MessageBatch<string>, env: Env): Promise<void> {
  for (let message of batch.messages) {
```

First, the queue function is defined, accepting a MessageBatch where the body of the messages are strings, as the producer on the Pages project provides a UUID in the message payload. The environment is provided too, so the function has access to the bindings it needs.

Next, the function begins to loop over the messages in the batch. Each message conforms to the Message interface, which looks like so:

```
interface Message<Body = unknown> {
  readonly id: string;
  readonly timestamp: Date;
  readonly body: Body;
  ack(): void;
  retry(): void;
}
```

The id is a unique system-generated ID from Cloudflare, timestamp lets you know when the message was published and body contains whatever data you published in the message. We'll cover the two methods ack() and retry() shortly.

```
const image_id = message.body
const image = await env.IMAGE_APP_UPLOADS.get(image_id);

if (image === null) {
  console.log(`Could not find image ID ${image_id}`);

  message.retry();
  continue;
}
```

Inside the loop, the function first needs to extract the UUID of the image from the message body. The Pages project stores the actual image in an R2 bucket, using a UUID for its name. Therefore, using the UUID from the message body, you can retrieve the image from R2.

To showcase how you can retry individual messages that fail, the final few lines of that section feature a little error handling. In the event that the image cannot be retrieved from R2, an error will be logged, and the retry method is called on the message.

Using the retry method, on a single message, allows you to instruct Cloudflare to retry just that message, and then you can continue on with the other messages in the batch. If there was no error handling here, the code later in the function would raise an error, then that message plus any other messages later in the batch would be marked as failed and retried, plus any prior messages that haven't been explicitly acknowledged using ack().

In the last section, we'll see ack() used too:

```
const inputs = {
  image: Array.from(
    new Uint8Array(await image.arrayBuffer())
  )
};
```

```
const analysis = await env.AI.run('@cf/microsoft/resnet-50', inputs);

await env.DB
  .prepare(
    'UPDATE images SET completed = 1, analysis = ?1 WHERE id = ?2'
  )
  .bind(JSON.stringify(analysis), image_id)
  .run();

await env.IMAGE_APP_UPLOADS.delete(image_id);

message.ack();
```

Before you can ack a message though, the image needs to be analyzed by the ResNet-50 model, which is exactly the same as in the Pages project. The only slight difference is the image is being pulled from R2, rather than the image being uploaded from the browser. Once the analysis is complete, you need to update the database to store the analysis, and mark the image as completed.

When you implement the changes to the front end to poll for image analysis, it'll query for an image that has analysis before it shows the analysis on the front end.

Lastly, the function explicitly acknowledges the message as processed using ack(). While you don't need to explicitly acknowledge a message as processed, it prevents a message that has been successfully processed being re-processed, which may cause issues with non-idempotent consumers (e.g. they're not safe to run multiple times for the same message).

If you don't explicitly ack() messages, then if all messages in a batch are successfully processed (no errors are raised), then the entire batch will be deemed successfully processed and removed from the queue. However, if any message in the batch fails, and no prior messages have been acknowledged, then all the messages in the batch will be retried.

Generally speaking, I'd always explicitly retry() and ack() messages individually where possible.

That's all that's needed for the consumer, as it's quite simple. For the application to work end to end, the front end portion needs updating to poll for the results, and show the results when the polling returns any new analysis.

Message Delivery and Guarantees

In the context of queues, it's common to have the ability to define the order in which messages are read. The most prevalent approach is "first in, first out" (FIFO), where older messages are processed first, and the latest message must wait until all the preceding messages are processed. Alternatively, "last in, first out" (LIFO) processes newer messages first, with older messages waiting longer.

At the time of writing, there are no strict ordering guarantees for the queues on Cloudflare, but it works as a FIFO queue. I suspect in future there'll be other types of ordering supported, as well as ordering guarantees, such that messages are guaranteed to be processed in the order they are published.

 Regarding delivery guarantees, Cloudflare ensures "at least once" delivery when a message is successfully published to a queue. This ensures that once a message is published, Cloudflare guarantees its delivery to your consumer at least once. Although the message is usually delivered only once, there might be rare instances of the same message being delivered twice.

This occurrence is common in asynchronous architecture, emphasizing the importance of ensuring that consumers are idempotent. Idempotency ensures that there are no unintended side effects if the same code is executed multiple times. For instance, if a consumer is responsible for actions like sending emails or processing payments, it's crucial to maintain records of emails sent or payments processed and verify that the same action hasn't already occurred before processing each message.

Poll for Analysis

After image processing, the consumer marks the corresponding database row as completed. To enable the front end to display the analysis results, you need to implement an endpoint that the front end polls for the analysis of user-uploaded images.

Asynchronous processing offers the benefit of progressively receiving analysis results as each message is processed. For instance, if ten images are uploaded, the front end can update results one by one or in small batches as they become available, eliminating the need to wait for all images to finish processing before displaying the analysis.

Upon image upload, the front end polls the new endpoint every two seconds, supplying UUIDs from the response of the POST /api/files endpoint as query string parameters.

To create the endpoint for the front end to poll, open up frontend/src/app/api/files/route.ts and add the following to the end of the file:

```
import retrieveImageAnalysisQuery from "@/lib/retrieve_image_analysis_query";

export async function GET(request: Request) {
  const url = new URL(request.url);
  const searchParams = new URLSearchParams(url.search);
  let image_ids = searchParams.get("image_ids")?.split(',')

  if (!image_ids) {
    return new Response('Image IDs not provided', {
      status: 404
    });
  }

  const all_results = await retrieveImageAnalysisQuery(image_ids);

  if (all_results.length === 0) {
    return new Response('Images not found', {
      status: 404
    });
  }

  let image_analysis = [];

  for (let x = 0; x < all_results.length; x++) {
    const row = all_results[x];

    image_analysis.push(
      {
        id: row.id,
        analysis: row.analysis ?
          JSON.parse(row.analysis as string) :
          false
      }
    )
  }

  return new Response(JSON.stringify(image_analysis), {
    headers: { 'content-type': 'application/json' }
  });
}
```

You should now have two functions in this file: one for the POST endpoint that handles image uploads, and the new GET endpoint to handle the front end polling for image analysis results. As always, let's break the code down piece by piece:

```
const url = new URL(request.url);
const searchParams = new URLSearchParams(url.search);
let image_ids = searchParams.get("image_ids")?.split(',')

if (!image_ids) {
  return new Response('Image IDs not provided', {
    status: 404
  });
}
```

The endpoint will be passed a comma-delimited list of image IDs to retrieve analysis for, for example, GET /api/files?image_ids=1,2,3. Therefore, the first thing the function does is retrieve the image_ids query string parameter and create an array, breaking the query string parameter up based on a comma. In the event no image IDs are provided, the endpoint returns a 404.

```
const all_results = await retrieveImageAnalysisQuery(image_ids);

if (all_results.length === 0) {
  return new Response('Images not found', {
    status: 404
  });
}
```

Next, the function calls a yet-to-be-defined function named retrieveImageAnalysis-Query. This function will be responsible for querying the data from the database, and to keep the endpoint itself relatively small, I extracted it to a separate function. We'll add it shortly.

```
let image_analysis = [];

for (let x = 0; x < all_results.length; x++) {
  const row = all_results[x];

  image_analysis.push(
    {
      id: row.id,
      analysis: row.analysis ?
        JSON.parse(row.analysis as string) :
        false
    }
  )
}

return new Response(JSON.stringify(image_analysis), {
  headers: { 'content-type': 'application/json' }
});
```

Lastly, the function prepares and returns a response to the front end by looping over each row returned from the database, and determining if image analysis is available or not. If it is, it's included in the response under the analysis property, else the property is set to false.

Before the endpoint will work, it needs the retrieveImageAnalysisQuery function to be implemented. Create a new file at frontend/src/lib/retrieve_image_analysis_query.ts and insert the following code:

```
import { getRequestContext } from '@cloudflare/next-on-pages';

type ImageQueryResult = {
  id: string,
  analysis: string,
  completed: number
}

const retrieveImageAnalysisQuery = async(
  image_ids: string[]
): Promise<Array<ImageQueryResult>> => {
  let imageAnalysis = new Array<ImageQueryResult>();
  const db = getRequestContext().env.DB;

  for (let x = 0; x < image_ids.length; x++) {
    const result = await db.prepare(
      'SELECT id, analysis, completed FROM images WHERE id IN (?1)'
    ).bind(image_ids[x])
     .first() as ImageQueryResult;

    imageAnalysis.push(
      {
        id: result.id,
        analysis: result.analysis,
        completed: result.completed
      }
    );
  }

  return imageAnalysis;
}

export default retrieveImageAnalysisQuery;
```

The function is simple, iterating through provided image UUIDs, fetching each image's state from the database, and returning the states in an array.

The last aspect that needs updating is the front end code itself, which isn't currently polling for any image analysis. The code for the front end is getting a little busy in one file, so before implementing the polling, let's extract some functionality to separate functions.

It's common in React is to define hooks that are effectively reusable functions. In this case, you don't need to reuse them, at least at this point, but it's a nice pattern to follow to simplify your code by extracting code to functions.

The current code in src/app/page.tsx handles the file upload, so let's move the majority of that file upload functionality to a hook in frontend/src/hooks/use_handle_image_upload.ts:

```
type ImageUploadResult = {
  id: string,
  filename: string
}

const useFileUpload = async(files: FileList) => {
  let uploadedImages: Array<UserImage> = [];

  if (files == undefined || files.length === 0) {
    return;
  }

  let formData = new FormData();

  for (let x = 0; x < files.length; x++) {
    formData.append('files', files[x]);

    uploadedImages.push(
      {
        url: URL.createObjectURL(files[x]),
        filename: files[x].name
      }
    )
  }

  const headers = {
    'content-type': "multipart/form-data"
  };

  await fetch("/api/files", { body: formData, method: "post"})
    .then(response => response.json<ImageUploadResult[]>())
    .then(response => {
      for(let x = 0; x < response.length; x++) {
        let image = uploadedImages.find(
          i => i.filename === response[x].filename
        )
        if (image) {
          image.id = response[x].id
        }
      }
    })

  return uploadedImages;
}

export default useFileUpload;
```

I won't go over the code in this one, as it's just been moved from the page's code. You'll need to amend a type though in frontend/additional.d.ts, updating UserImage to the following:

```
interface UserImage {
    filename: string;
    url: string;
    analysis?: Array<Analysis>;
    id?: string;
}
```

All that's changed here is we added an optional field id that'll be used to track the ID of the file that's uploaded; it's effectively the ID that's stored in the database.

To keep things consistent, let's create a second hook to handle the polling. Create a second file at frontend/src/hooks/use_poll_for_analysis.ts.

```
type ImageAnalysisResponse = {
  id: string,
  analysis: Analysis[]
}
const usePollForAnalysis = async(uploadedImages: Array<UserImage>) => {
  const image_ids = uploadedImages.map(x => x.id)

  await fetch(`/api/files?image_ids=${image_ids.join()}`)
    .then(response => response.json<Array<ImageAnalysisResponse>>())
    .then(response => {
      for (let x = 0; x < response.length; x++) {
        if (!response[x].analysis) {
          continue;
        }

        let image = uploadedImages.find(
          i => i.id === response[x].id
        )

        if (image) {
          image.analysis = response[x].analysis;
        }
      }
    })

  return uploadedImages;
}

export default usePollForAnalysis;
```

The function will be passed an array of UserImages, which represent the images that were uploaded by the user. The IDs are extracted from that array, and the server-side endpoint you just created will be called using the IDs.

Once a response is returned, the function attempts to match any image analysis returned from the API call to the images the user uploaded. This is easy enough to do, as both the UserImage and the API response contain the image IDs, so they can be used to match the analysis to the images.

The hooks the front end needs to function now exist, so there's one final file to change. The page itself needs updating to use the hooks, along with a couple of other tweaks. Open frontend/src/app/page.tsx and replace the code at the top of the file, up until the return starts that provides the HTML for the front end.

```
'use client';

import React, { useRef } from "react";
import { ChangeEvent } from "react";
import { ImageList } from "@/components/ImageList";
import useFileUpload from "@/hooks/use_handle_image_upload";
import usePollForAnalysis from "@/hooks/use_poll_for_analysis";

export default function Home() {
  const intervalRef = useRef(0);

  const handleChange = async (event: ChangeEvent) => {
    const files = (event.target as HTMLInputElement).files;

    if (!files) {
      return;
    }

    // eslint-disable-next-line react-hooks/rules-of-hooks
    const uploadedImages = await useFileUpload(files);

    if (uploadedImages) {
      setUploadedImages(uploadedImages);

      intervalRef.current = window.setInterval(
        pollForAnalysis,
        2000,
        uploadedImages
      );
    }
  }

  const pollForAnalysis = async(uploadedImages: Array<UserImage>) => {
    // eslint-disable-next-line react-hooks/rules-of-hooks
    const imagesWithAnalysis = await usePollForAnalysis(uploadedImages);

    if (imagesWithAnalysis.every(i => i.analysis)) {
      window.clearInterval(intervalRef.current);
```

```
  }
  setUploadedImages([...imagesWithAnalysis]);
}

const [uploadedImages, setUploadedImages] = React.useState(
  new Array<UserImage>()
);
```

The file itself looks a lot cleaner with the primary functionality extracted to hooks, and in terms of behavior, it's largely the same. There's a few things worth calling out though:

```
const intervalRef = useRef(0);
```

At the very top of the function, you make use of useRef, which is a hook built into React. It allows you to store a value that persists between renders, but it's a really simple way to store a single value. You'll need it later to enable the front end to stop polling when all the image analysis is rendered.

```
if (uploadedImages) {
  setUploadedImages(uploadedImages);

  intervalRef.current = window.setInterval(
    pollForAnalysis,
    2000,
    uploadedImages
  );
}
```

When the images are uploaded by a user, the images are set in React's state as before, but as the analysis isn't returned from the API that handles image uploads, there's an additional step of setting an interval to poll for analysis. In JavaScript, setInterval will call a given function (first parameter) at a defined interval (second parameter), passing any arguments needed (third parameter). Effectively, once the images have been uploaded, the browser will poll for image analysis every two seconds.

Lastly, the pollForImageAnalysis function that will be called every two seconds:

```
const pollForAnalysis = async(uploadedImages: Array<UserImage>) => {
  // eslint-disable-next-line react-hooks/rules-of-hooks
  const imagesWithAnalysis = await usePollForAnalysis(uploadedImages);

  if (imagesWithAnalysis.every(i => i.analysis)) {
    window.clearInterval(intervalRef.current);
  }

  setUploadedImages([...imagesWithAnalysis]);
}
```

This function makes use of the usePollForAnalysis hook you created earlier. If the function detects that all images have analysis, it clears the interval so the API endpoint is no longer polled, as there is no need. Before productionizing the application, you would probably want to have some way to stop polling for analysis after a given amount of time, to account for errors, and a lot of wasted API calls.

Lastly, it updates React's state with the images with analysis. The ellipsis (...) effectively makes a copy of the array, as React's state will only be updated if the value has changed. As only the analysis key changes within each object in the array, the state wouldn't get updated, so you force it by creating a new array, and coping imagesWithAnalysis into it.

Those are the final changes that are needed, so go ahead and test everything is working as you expect.

Test the Consumer

Unlike previous projects, this application requires two separate deployments, even though they share a version control repository.

Start by deploying the consumer. Navigate to the image-analysis-consumer folder and execute npm run deploy. Once completed, go to the frontend folder and run npm run deploy. Unfortunately, at present, you can't run your producer and consumer locally if they are in different Workers. This is marked as a known issue in the Cloudflare documentation, so hopefully in the future this is resolved. For now, you'll need to deploy when using Queues in separate projects.

After both deployments, visit the URL provided in the front end deployment output. Upload a couple of small images, avoiding large megabyte-sized ones, as the AI model handles smaller sizes more effectively.

If everything goes well, you'll observe the gradual rendering of image analysis results on the screen.

What You've Learned

We're at the end of another chapter, which means it's time for a recap of what you've learned.

You learned how to create a consumer to process messages in asynchronous workflows, including what is a consumer, what is a queue, and how to set those two up in Cloudflare. On top of that, you learned about batches, retries, and how you can tweak the concurrency of your consumers.

Although you've used bindings several times now, you made use of them again when building the consumer to communicate with several services: D1, R2, and an AI model, so you consolidated some learning there, too.

The full code for both the Pages project and the Worker are available on GitHub.[1,2]

This is the last chapter on Queues, and the next chapter is something completely different from anything you've likely seen before. Wouldn't it be cool if you could store the objects in your code in persistence storage? That's exactly what you'll learn next, taking a close look at what Cloudflare calls Durable Objects.

Queues Pricing

Queues pricing is straightforward; you're charged for the number of messages processed. Queues are only available on the $5 Workers Paid plan, with one million operations included per month. Operations include write, read, and delete. Therefore, to write a single message to a queue, read it, and then delete it, takes three operations. Retries will incur additional read operations.

Beyond the included limit, you'll be charged $0.40 per million operations.

1. https://github.com/apeacock1991/serverless-apps-on-cloudflare/tree/main/image-app-with-queue-producer
2. https://github.com/apeacock1991/serverless-apps-on-cloudflare/tree/main/image-analysis-consumer

## CHAPTER 13

WebSockets with Durable Objects

If you have prior experience building web applications, a lot of the core building blocks we've explored so far, such as databases and caches, will be familiar to you. As you progressed through the book, you learned how to use those building blocks specifically on the Cloudflare platform and in a serverless environment.

Before we dive into the project for this chapter, let's consider a use case we haven't yet covered in the book: real-time applications. These are the kinds of applications that feel incredibly responsive and almost alive. For example, a multiplayer game such as Clash of Clans, real-time chat such as Discord, collaborating on a shared document in Google Docs, or drawing out a mind map in Miro.

All of these have real-time elements to them, where you can see input from other users almost as if they were in the same room as you. Unsurprisingly, they are also one of the most complex types of application to build.

One of the key ingredients to a real-time application is often WebSockets, a completely different protocol to HTTP. All the applications so far made use of the HTTP protocol, where a client makes a request to a server, and waits for a response. This is often referred to as unidirectional communication.

Compare that to WebSockets, which are bidirectional. Once the connection between a client and server is established, both client and server can send messages to one another whenever they like—there is no concept of requests and responses like in HTTP, just messages exchanged between the two parties. The connection between the client and the server is maintained for as long as is needed, effectively until one side closes the connection.

As you can imagine, this lends itself well to real-time use cases. Take a chat application. Once the client is connected to the chat that is being handled by the server, new messages can be sent freely whenever they are available. If you tried to do the same with HTTP—which is definitely possible—you'd need some sort of polling mechanism, which will be much slower, less responsive, and a lot less efficient. If you took the complexity up a notch, to a game for example, it wouldn't be feasible to be constantly polling the server for the latest game state. It would be too slow and the experience too choppy.

In this chapter, regardless of your level of experience or length of time as an engineer, I almost guarantee you've never seen or worked with anything that makes these kinds of use cases so effortless—or really, ever seen anything like this, period.

Cloudflare calls them Durable Objects. In effect, imagine you create an object in your code to represent something—be it a chat room or a game—and it holds the state for that thing. This is as simple as const chat = new Chat() in JavaScript. If you create that object when an HTTP request is received, it'll remain in memory while your code handles the request, and then it'll be removed.

If you want to maintain state between requests, this is often handled by a database. Continuing the chat example, you would store any messages in the database and load those messages into the Chat object when needed.

Durable Objects simplify this pattern by effectively allowing you to persist regular JavaScript objects on Cloudflare's platform, including the state held by that object. Cloudflare guarantees there'll only ever be one instance of your Durable Object at any point in time, and you request that Durable Object from Cloudflare whenever you need it.

To get to grips with Durable Objects and WebSockets, you're going to create a simple chat application. It'll feature a simple interface that allows anyone to enter their name to join a chat, then share that link for others to join. The messages sent for a given chat will be persisted so they're not lost if the page is refreshed, and anyone joining the chat late can see the messages sent prior.

Create a Worker with Durable Objects

First, you need to create a new project. I'm sure you know the drill by now:

```
$ npm create cloudflare@2.21.1 -- --no-auto-update
```

For the prompts, select the following:

- chat-app for the project name
- "Hello World" Durable Object, when prompted for the type of application

- Yes to TypeScript
- Yes to Git for version control
- Don't deploy the application for now

After a few seconds, Cloudflare will create a brand new project, complete with an example Durable Object. The structure should look familiar to you, as this is mostly just a Worker for now. However, in src/index.ts, there are some new concepts to go over:

```
import { DurableObject } from "cloudflare:workers";

export interface Env {
  MY_DURABLE_OBJECT: DurableObjectNamespace<MyDurableObject>;
}

export class MyDurableObject extends DurableObject {
  constructor(ctx: DurableObjectState, env: Env) {
    super(ctx, env);
  }

  async sayHello(name: string): Promise<string> {
    return `Hello, ${name}!`;
  }
}

export default {
  async fetch(request, env, ctx): Promise<Response> {
    let id: DurableObjectId = env.MY_DURABLE_OBJECT.idFromName(
      new URL(request.url).pathname
    );

    let stub = env.MY_DURABLE_OBJECT.get(id);

    let greeting = await stub.sayHello("world");

    return new Response(greeting);
  },
}
```

Starting from the top, the DurableObject abstract class is imported, which is used later on to create your own Durable Objects. Following that, there's the environment definition where you need to list the bindings so that your Worker has access to create Durable Objects. Unlike D1, KV, and others, you don't need to create specific resources such as tables and namespaces ahead of time. Instead, the Worker itself creates new instances of Durable Objects as it needs.

Next, a new Durable Object is defined by exporting a class that extends the DurableObject abstract class. (The code starts on the next page.)

```
export class MyDurableObject extends DurableObject {
  constructor(ctx: DurableObjectState, env: Env) {
    super(ctx, env);
  }

  async sayHello(name: string): Promise<string> {
    return `Hello, ${name}!`;
  }
}
```

As explained in the introduction, Durable Objects look just like regular classes. Firstly, they have a constructor, with two arguments passed:

- ctx, which is short for context, gives you access to a number of methods that are specific to Durable Objects to help you manage its lifecycle. For example, Durable Objects come with a built-in key-value store, which can be accessed in this context.

- env should be very familiar to you now, which represents the environment for your Durable Object, giving it access to bindings and secrets.

Secondly, you can define methods on Durable Objects as you would any other class. In the code above, a simple sayHello method is defined that does some simple string interpolation. This is how you add behavior to your Durable Objects.

With the Durable Object defined, the Worker can now interact with it when an HTTP request is received:

```
export default {
  async fetch(request, env, ctx): Promise<Response> {
    let id: DurableObjectId = env.MY_DURABLE_OBJECT.idFromName(
      new URL(request.url).pathname
    );

    let stub = env.MY_DURABLE_OBJECT.get(id);

    let greeting = await stub.sayHello("world");

    return new Response(greeting);
  },
}
```

We'll get into the different ways you can interact with a Durable Object later in the chapter, but for now, you can at least see that you use bindings to make use of Durable Objects.

As Durable Objects are represented in your code as classes, that means you can call methods on them in the same way you would any other class. In the code above, once the Durable Object is retrieved, the sayHello method is called.

When working with standard classes, this would call the method of a class in memory, all happening on the same machine.

However, when calling a method on a Durable Object, even though it looks like a local method call, it's being executed using Remote Procedure Call (RPC) against the Durable Object. The code in your Worker interacts with a stub, a proxy if you like, that provides a simple and familiar interface for you to use in the form of classes.

With the basic code explained, let's dive into creating the chat application using Durable Objects. To begin, we'll need a simple chat interface.

Serve HTML from a Worker

In Chapter 6, Build a Static Website with Pages, on page 65, and Chapter 9, Upload and Store Files on R2, on page 113, you used Cloudflare Pages to build and deploy your front end. However, it's possible to serve HTML from a Worker to act as your front end using Static Assets Workers.[1] In the same way you used Cloudflare Pages to build a full-stack application using Next.js, you can do the same with Static Assets Workers, too. Don't be fooled by the name: building dynamic websites is absolutely possible.[2]

You aren't going to use Next.js here, to keep things a bit simpler. You'll need the HTML itself, which I'm not going to include directly here as it's too long, but it's available to download alongside all the code in this book. You'll find it named 13-app.html. This is what it would look like once rendered:

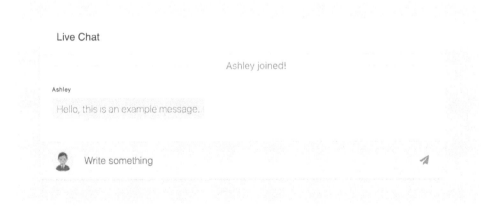

---

1. To use the new Static Assets Workers, you must be on Wrangler 3.78.10 or later; run npm install wrangler@3.78.10 to be sure.
2. https://developers.cloudflare.com/workers/frameworks/

The initial page load contains an input box where the user enters their name, and once they submit, they're presented with this screen. I'll go over the JavaScript needed to interact with the back end for the chat, but we'll tackle that at the end.

Once you've downloaded the source files provided alongside the book, retrieve the HTML from 13-app.html and store it in a new file under public/index.html.

As Workers don't have access to the file system during runtime, you can't just load the HTML from the file and serve it. Instead, you can configure the Worker to be able to serve static assets from a specific folder by editing the wrangler.toml file:

```
compatibility_date = "2024-09-25"
assets = { directory = "./public/" }
```

First, you need to update the compatibility date to a more recent one if it's not set to the date above. The compatibility date effectively determines what version of the Workers runtime you use, and as Static Assets Workers are very new at the time of writing, you may need to use a newer version of the runtime than what was set when the project was created.

Second, you define a directory where your static assets will be served from. When a request comes into a Worker with assets defined, it first checks to see if the path requested matches a static asset; if it does, that'll be returned. If no matches are found, it'll execute the fetch method of your Worker. More information on routing can be found in the docs.[3]

You don't need to for this application, but you can optionally set a binding that allows you to programmatically access assets:

```
assets = { directory = "./public/", binding = "ASSETS" }
```

You can then dynamically access assets from your Worker if you need to, using env.ASSETS.fetch(request). You could use this to return a different image from the assets directory for the same path, based on HTTP headers or other data points. Maybe you have different variations of your logo you want to serve based on the country of origin, for example.

The Worker can now return static assets, but for the API, we'll need to make use of the fetch function of the Worker. You'll make use of itty-router once more to handle routing; add it to your project's dependencies by running:

```
$ npm install --save itty-router
```

---

3. https://developers.cloudflare.com/workers/static-assets/routing/

Let's create the basic code needed to serve routes next. Import the necessary dependencies from itty-router, create the Router and add its one route to render HTML in src/index.ts below the line that imports the DurableObject class:

```
import {
  error,
  Router,
} from 'itty-router'

const router = Router();

router
  .all('*', () => error(404))
```

Lastly, update the fetch method like so:

```
export default {
  async fetch(
    request: Request,
    env: Env,
    ctx: ExecutionContext
  ): Promise<Response> {
    return router.fetch(request, env);
  },
};
```

The two exports, Env and MyDurableObject, are technically superfluous for now—but don't remove them yet, we'll do so later in the chapter.

You can validate the HTML is being rendered by running your Worker with npm run dev and accessing the URL given by Wrangler in the output. You can type your name in the box and hit the button, and the page should update to say it's connecting to chat.

There's no back end logic yet to handle chats, and if you look in your terminal where your Worker is running, you'll see a 404 returned for /api/chat. When a new chat is created, or someone joins an existing chat, that's the endpoint that is hit, so you'll implement that next.

Create Durable Objects

Before you can create the Durable Object class, you need to add the API endpoint /api/chat that will interact with the Durable Object. Open src/index.ts and add the following to the Router configuration—make sure it goes above .all:

```
.get('/api/chat', (request: Request, env: Env) => {
  const chatId = new URL(request.url).searchParams.get('chatId')

  if (!chatId) {
    return new Response("Chat ID is missing", {status: 400});
  }
```

```
  const doId = env.CHATS.idFromName(chatId);
  const chat = env.CHATS.get(doId);
  if (request.headers.get("Upgrade") != "websocket") {
    return new Response("expected websocket", {status: 400});
  }

  return chat.fetch(request.clone());
})
```

Let's step through the code section by section. First, the endpoint retrieves and validates that a chat ID has been passed:

```
.get('/api/chat', (request: Request, env: Env) => {
  const chatId = new URL(request.url).searchParams.get('chatId')

  if (!chatId) {
    return new Response("Chat ID is missing", {status: 400});
  }
```

This is essential, as each chat will be stored in its own Durable Object. When the front end requests to create or join a chat, it'll pass a unique identifier in the form of a UUID. This UUID is then used to find or create a Durable Object:

```
const doId = env.CHATS.idFromName(chatId);
const chat = env.CHATS.get(doId);
```

You haven't configured the binding yet, but the Durable Object will be accessible in the environment in the same way any other binding is. There's no need to create resources, as Durable Objects are created dynamically by code. The binding simply maps from the name used in your code, in this case CHATS, to a class, which you'll add later.

There could be ten thousand chats happening, perhaps simultaneously, so when a user connects to a chat, you need a way to consistently retrieve the correct Durable Object. There are a few methods you can interact with on the binding to achieve this:

1. idFromName allows you to pass a string and return a unique Durable Object ID. The method is deterministic, so given the same string, you're always guaranteed to get the same ID back. For example, if you wanted to create one global chat, you could hard-code this to env.CHATS.isFromName('global') instead of passing the UUID of the chat.

2. newUniqueId generates a new unique Durable Object ID, which you then need to store somewhere to retrieve the same Durable Object when needed. This is done by calling toString on the returned value, which converts the ID to a hexadecimal string. To retrieve the Durable Object later, you pass that hexadecimal string to idFromString.

In an ideal world, the code above would use newUniqueId and return the output of toString to the front end, rather than the front end passing in a UUID. It requires a little more work though, so to keep the code simple. The front end is responsible for generating the UUID and storing it in the URL in the browser.

Lastly, the endpoint checks that the incoming request seeks to establish a WebSocket connection. If so, it offloads the responsibility of creating the WebSocket connection to the Durable Object by calling its fetch method:

```
if (request.headers.get("Upgrade") != "websocket") {
  return new Response("expected websocket", {status: 400});
}

return chat.fetch(request.clone());
```

When establishing a new WebSocket connection, the client must request to upgrade, as WebSockets use their own protocol, rather than HTTP. If the client isn't seeking to establish a WebSocket connection, the endpoint returns an error.

If the client is establishing a WebSocket connection, the endpoint calls the fetch method of a to-be-defined Durable Object which will return an appropriate response to establish such a connection.

The client can now call /api/chat to connect to a new chat, but the Durable Object needed to handle the WebSockets doesn't exist yet—you'll add that now.

Connect to WebSockets with Durable Objects

If you weren't using Cloudflare, this is where things would likely get more complex. You would need to source a library or framework for handling WebSockets, as well as handle the full lifecycle of each connection. With Cloudflare, though, it's going to do all the heavy lifting for you, alongside some cost-saving measures we'll cover later.

In terms of code, Durable Objects are defined as regular classes. Let's define the Durable Object that's going to handle your WebSocket connections by creating a new file at src/chat.ts containing the following:

```
import { DurableObject } from "cloudflare:workers";

type RawUserMessage = {
  text: string;
  name: string;
  connection_established?: boolean;
}
```

```
type FormattedUserMessage = {
  text: string;
  type: string;
  name?: string;
}

export class Chat extends DurableObject {
  constructor(ctx: DurableObjectState, env: any) {
    super(ctx, env);
  }
  async fetch(request: Request) {
    let [client, server] = Object.values(new WebSocketPair());
    this.ctx.acceptWebSocket(server);

    return new Response(null, { status: 101, webSocket: client });
  }
}
```

That's all the code necessary to enable a Durable Object to accept incoming WebSocket connections. Although there isn't a lot, there are lots of things going on here, so let's step through piece by piece.

```
import { DurableObject } from "cloudflare:workers";

type RawUserMessage = {
  text: string;
  name: string;
  connection_established?: boolean;
}

type FormattedUserMessage = {
  text: string;
  type: string;
  name?: string;
}

export class Chat extends DurableObject {
  constructor(ctx: DurableObjectState, env: any) {
    super(ctx, env);
  }
```

First, whenever you want to define a Durable Object, you need to import the DurableObject abstract class from the @cloudflare/workers-types package. Below that import, two types are defined that will be used later—one to represent the messages coming in from the front end, and another to represent messages parsed for the back end to understand.

After that, you can see a class named Chat being exported that extends the DurableObject class.

By extending the DurableObject class, the classes you define get access to the key features Durable Objects provide, such as handling for WebSockets. When a new Durable Object is created, its constructor will be called, the same as any other class. At the very least, you should call the parent class's constructor by calling super, which sets the state and environment in the class's properties. You can then execute any code you need after calling super.

The Durable Object gets access to the same environment as the Worker that created them, giving you access to bindings and secrets in the same way a Worker does. Additionally, Cloudflare passes some context to the constructor with the type DurableObjectState.

This context, shortened in the code to ctx, is quite vaguely named, but that's because it provides access to so many different APIs:

- *Alarms* are effectively scheduled tasks, allowing you to define a set time in the future when the Durable Object will be executed.

- *Transactional storage* does what it says on the tin. It gives each instance of a Durable Worker access to its own key-value store.

- *WebSockets* we'll cover extensively in this chapter, with a number of functions provided by the context to interact with them.

- *WebGPU* is an experimental API, that's only available locally at present, but in future, you'll be able to access a GPU from a Durable Object.

You won't be using alarms or GPUs in this book, but you'll make use of the transactional storage and WebSocket APIs. If want to try the others out, Cloudflare's documentation covers them.[4]

After the constructor, a fetch method is defined:

```
async fetch(request: Request) {
  let [client, server] = Object.values(new WebSocketPair());
  this.ctx.acceptWebSocket(server);

  return new Response(null, { status: 101, webSocket: client });
}
```

This method is responsible for opening the WebSocket connection, and returning it to the client. When communicating via WebSockets, each connection has two parties: a client and a server. In order for one party to send a message to the other, the client WebSocket will be sent back to the browser, and the server, which is implemented by the Durable Object, will retain the server side of the WebSocket.

---

4.   https://developers.cloudflare.com/durable-objects/api/

This allows each party to communicate with each other at will, as a message sent by the client will be received by the server, and vice-versa. The client and server WebSockets are created using WebSocketPair.

Before returning the client WebSocket, the server must first accept the Web-Socket connection to enable it to start sending and receiving messages. This is done by calling acceptWebSocket on the context provided by Cloudflare in the constructor. Behind the scenes, this causes a handshake to happen, in the same way a browser does an SSL handshake.

If you're interested in the finer details, Mozilla has an excellent in-depth and low-level guide to WebSocket servers.[5] For our purposes, all we need to know is that before WebSocket messages can be exchanged, you need to call this.ctx.acceptWebSocket(server) and Cloudflare will handle the underlying complexities for you.

WebSocket Hibernation

Due to the serverless nature of Cloudflare's platform, you only pay for what you use. When it comes to WebSockets, you might expect this would quickly become expensive, as surely the Durable Object is present in memory whenever a client is connected?

Fortunately, this is not the case. When calling acceptWebSocket() within a Durable Object, Cloudflare is able to hibernate the Durable Object between messages. Effectively, this means the Durable Object can be evicted from memory, and is no longer running, unless messages are being handled.

The WebSocket connection isn't closed though, and remains open. Then, when a message is received, the Durable Object will be loaded into memory to handle the incoming message. Any data stored using its transactional storage will be saved, but any custom properties on the class will be lost. When a Durable Object is loaded after hibernation, the constructor is called, so you can easily reset any properties.

At this point, once the client accepts the WebSocket connection too, messages are able to be sent and received between the client and the server. However, in order for the Durable Object to handle incoming messages, you must define a method to do so.

---

5.   https://developer.mozilla.org/en-US/docs/Web/API/WebSockets_API/Writing_WebSocket_servers

Handle Server-Side WebSocket Messages

Your Durable Object is now able to create WebSocket connections. It would now be possible to connect from both the client and server, but as of yet, no messages are being exchanged.

Durable Objects provide a simple interface for handling a number of WebSocket-related features, with the most common being able to receive a message.

In src/chat.ts, add the following four methods below the constructor:

```
async webSocketMessage(ws: WebSocket, message:  string) {
  const user_message = this.formatUserMessage(message);
  this.broadcastMessage(user_message);
}

async webSocketClose(
  ws: WebSocket,
  code: number,
  reason: string,
  wasClean: boolean
) {
  ws.close(code, "Durable Object is closing WebSocket");
}

broadcastMessage(user_message: FormattedUserMessage) {
  const websockets = this.ctx.getWebSockets()

  for(let x = 0; x < websockets.length; x++) {
    const session = websockets[x];
    session.send(JSON.stringify(user_message));
  }
}

formatUserMessage(websocket_message: string): FormattedUserMessage {
  const data = JSON.parse(websocket_message) as RawUserMessage;
  let user_message;

  if (data.connection_established) {
    user_message = {
      text: `${data.name} joined!`,
      type: 'metadata'
    }
  } else {
    user_message = {
      text: data.text,
      name: data.name,
      type: 'user_message'
    }
  }

  return user_message;
}
```

You can think of the first two methods as event handlers that are triggered in certain scenarios, with the interface being defined by the DurableObject abstract class. The webSocketClose method is relatively self-explanatory, and is triggered whenever the client WebSocket disconnects. The most common case where this would happen is the end user closing their browser. If the client WebSocket is closed, you also close the WebSocket on the server side, as it's no longer possible to communicate with the client.

The webSocketMessage method is called when the server-side WebSocket receives a message from the client. Whenever a message is sent, the chat application needs to broadcast that message to everyone who's connected, so they see the message on their screen.

To do so, formatUserMessage is called to cater for two cases. The first is when someone new joins the chat; the browser will send a message saying they are connected, otherwise it's a regular message that just needs to be broadcast pretty much as is.

Once formatted, the message can be sent to anyone connected to the chat. This is handled by the broadcastMessage method, which has two very important parts to it.

Each time someone tries to connect to a chat, which is maintained by a specific Durable Object, acceptWebSocket is called. Not only does this enable the server-side WebSocket to receive messages, it also stores the WebSocket within the Durable Object, effectively building up a list of WebSockets.

You can get that list by calling this.ctx.getWebSockets(), which returns an array of connected WebSockets. When calling acceptWebSocket, you can pass an optional array of tags to help you group or identify specific WebSockets. You can then receive tag-specific WebSockets by passing the tag to this.ctx.getWebSockets(). If no tags are passed, then all connected WebSockets are returned.

Once the list of connected WebSockets has been retrieved, you can send the desired message to each one. To send a message to a WebSocket, you call the send method, and pass the message.

Before running the Worker and seeing your WebSockets in action, three tiny changes are needed elsewhere. First, open src/index.ts and add the following export at the top of the file:

```
export { Chat } from "./chat"
```

This exports the Chat class that's implemented as a Durable Object so that Cloudflare can import it. You should also remove the export for Env and the

MyDurableObject class from this file too. Next, open worker-configuration.d.ts and update it to the following:

```
interface Env {
  CHATS: DurableObjectNamespace;
}
```

This adds a binding to the environment interface, so that your Worker is able to access your Durable Object at runtime. Lastly, you need to add the configuration for the binding itself in wrangler.toml:

```
[[durable_objects.bindings]]
name = "CHATS"
class_name = "Chat"

[[migrations]]
tag = "v1"
new_classes = ["Chat"]
```

As Cloudflare creates a ton of comments showing all the possible bindings, I would remove everything in the file except the top-level keys, which are typically name, main, and compatibility_date, and then add the above.

Durable Object bindings are a little different from the other bindings you've used so far. Defining the actual binding is relatively familiar, with name being the reference you use in your code to access the Durable Object, alongside specifying the class_name, which should match the name of the class you export that implements your Durable Object.

However, with Durable Objects, there's an additional piece of configuration needed. When adding, renaming, or deleting classes that implement Durable Objects, you need a migration.

As you're adding a Durable Object for the first time, the migration simply specifies that a new class is added, and tags it with v1. If you want to rename the class in the future, or delete previously created Durable Objects, you must do a migration—you don't need to make this change in the application you're currently building:

```
[[migrations]]
tag = "v2"
renamed_classes = [
  { from = "CurrentDurableObject", to = "UpdatedDurableObject" }
]
deleted_classes = ["DeprecatedClass"] # Array of deleted class names
```

In the example above, which you should not put into your chat application, the class CurrentDurableObject was renamed to UpdatedDurableObject, so a migration was needed. This will ensure all data stored in any Durable Objects created by CurrentDurableObject is migrated to new Durable Objects that implement UpdatedDurableObject.

Along the same lines, if you no longer have a use for a Durable Object, you can delete it by specifying a migration with deleted_classes. When delete migration is run, all Durable Objects that implement the given class are deleted, including any storage associated with them.

With all the changes made, you can finally see your chat application in action. Run npm run dev and open the application in your browser. Type in your name, connect to the chat, and then you'll be able to send messages and see them rendered on your screen. Note: out of habit, you might press enter to send a message, but to save on the amount of code needed, there are no such events—you'll need to click the send icon.

It's not very representative to have just one person connected to the chat though, so you can copy the URL in the address bar, which will contain a chatId, and paste it into a new tab. Connect to the chat once again, and you should see any messages sent in one tab propagated to the chat window in the other tab in real time.

It works nicely, but you'll notice that if you refresh the page and reconnect to the chat, or you join the chat after messages have been sent, you don't see all the messages. At present, there's no storage of messages, which for some use cases might be totally fine—perhaps you don't want past messages to be accessible.

In this case, though, let's say you do want to persist messages for each chat; let's add that next.

Persist Data with Durable Objects

Alongside built-in support for WebSockets, Durable Objects come with their own storage. Each operation is wrapped in a transaction, making them isolated, atomic, and strongly consistent. Even though the instance of your Durable Object will be removed from memory when it isn't serving requests, any data stored using its transactional storage won't be lost. This is likely where the durable in Durable Objects comes from.

In terms of the chat application, you'll now implement the ability to see prior messages sent in the chat when joining. For example, if Harry joins and sends a message before Tom joins, Tom will be able to see the message Harry sent after joining.

Durable Object Pricing

Durable Objects are only available on the Workers Paid plan, currently priced at $5/month. You can still run through the code in this chapter locally without upgrading; you just won't be able to use any in production without the paid plan. With that plan, you get 1 million requests to Durable Objects included. If you exceed 1 million requests, you're charged $0.15 per additional million requests.

You're also billed for the amount of time your Durable Object is running, measured in GB seconds. You get 400,000 GB seconds included on the plan, with each additional million GB seconds charged at $12.50.

That might sound expensive, but even 400,000 GB-s can go a long way. Let's say your Durable Object is active for 1 million seconds in a month, which is roughly equivalent for 11.5 days. That would total 128,000 GB seconds, costing you nothing in that month.

Each Durable Object can use up to 128MB of memory, and you're charged on that amount rather than the actual memory usage. Therefore, to help explain the pricing, you would do the following to calculate usage: 1,000,000 seconds * 128 MB / 1 GB = 128,000 GB seconds.

Keep in mind that when using WebSockets, the Durable Objects will be hibernated when they aren't handling messages, meaning they don't rack up costs when they're idle.

The changes are relatively small, and are contained entirely in the Durable Object. Open src/chat.ts and add the following method to the bottom of the class:

```
async persistHistory(user_message: FormattedUserMessage) {
  let history = await this
    .ctx.storage.get<FormattedUserMessage[]>('message-history');

  if (!history) {
    await this.ctx.storage.put('message-history', [user_message]);
  } else {
    history.push(user_message);
    await this.ctx.storage.put('message-history', history);
  }
}
```

As the name indicates, this method is responsible for persisting a single message. It first retrieves any existing messages from storage that are stored under the key message-history, using this.ctx.storage.get. Following that, it determines whether any prior messages exist in storage. If there are, it appends the latest message, else it persists a new array containing the user message. In both cases, this.ctx.storage.put is used to store the given value under the specified key.

A common problem when dealing with data is ensuring that a series of reads and/or writes either all succeed, or all fail—this is often referred to as being atomic. In the case of Durable Objects, any series of reads and/or writes without any intervening I/O will automatically be atomic, so they effectively behave as if they are wrapped within a transaction.

With the logic for persisting message history complete, you can now call it whenever a new message is received. Update the webSocketMessage method like so:

```
async webSocketMessage(ws: WebSocket, message:  string) {
  const user_message = this.formatUserMessage(message);

  this.persistHistory(user_message);

  this.broadcastMessage(user_message);
}
```

All messages sent will now be stored by the Durable Object responsible for that chat. The only thing left to do is update the fetch method of the Durable Object to send all messages stored whenever a new client connects:

```
async fetch(request: Request) {
  let [client, server] = Object.values(new WebSocketPair());
  this.ctx.acceptWebSocket(server);

  this.ctx.storage.get<FormattedUserMessage[]>('message-history')
    .then(messages => {
      if (messages) {
        for(let x = 0; x < messages.length; x++) {
          server.send(JSON.stringify(messages[x]))
        }
      }
    })

  return new Response(null, { status: 101, webSocket: client });
}
```

After accepting a WebSocket, messages can be sent immediately. Making use of this.ctx.storage.get once more, all the messages stored by the Durable Object are retrieved and sent to the client that just joined in a similar fashion to when a message is broadcast.

Those are all the changes needed. You can see the changes in action by running npm run dev, opening the chat application in your browser, sending a few messages, and then refreshing the page. Once you enter your name again and submit the form, you'll see all the prior messages sent rendered on your screen.

Before summarizing what you've learned in this chapter, let's take a quick look at the client-side code needed to connect to a WebSocket.

SQLite Storage

Alongside a key-value store, you can use SQLite storage as well in Durable Objects. At the time of writing, this is in beta.[6]

You can run queries against that database using ctx.storage.sql.exec, including creating the initial tables. That might sound strange at first, as wouldn't that be slow? Not with SQLite in Durable Objects, as it's running in the same thread as your Durable Object, effectively giving you zero-latency queries.

While the key-value store is perfect for simple use cases, if you're storing a lot of data and need more structure around it, SQLite is going to be the answer.

Connect to WebSockets with JavaScript

Although the code is already included in your application, I wanted to quickly go over the JavaScript code needed on the client side to close the loop on WebSockets. I'll break it down into digestible sections. Here's the JavaScript code, written in jQuery, needed to establish a WebSocket connection and send messages:

```javascript
$(document).on('click', '#connect-btn', function() {
  const name = $('#connect-name').val();

  $('#connect-container').html('Connecting to chat...');

  let chat_id = new URLSearchParams(document.location.search).get('chatId');
  let hostname = window.location.host;
  const wss = document.location.protocol === "http:" ? "ws://" : "wss://";
  let connect_url = wss + hostname + `/api/chat?name=${name}`;

  if (!chat_id) {
    chat_id = crypto.randomUUID();
    window.history.pushState({}, '', `/?chatId=${chat_id}`);
  }
```

---

6.   https://blog.cloudflare.com/sqlite-in-durable-objects/

```
  connect_url += `&chatId=${chat_id}`

  let ws = new WebSocket(connect_url);
  $(document).on('click', '#send-msg-btn', function(e) {
    e.preventDefault();

    const msg = $('#chat-msg-input').val();

    ws.send(
      JSON.stringify({ text: msg, name: name })
    )

    $('#chat-msg-input').val('');
  })
});
```

Once the user types their name in and clicks the submit button, the client attempts to open a WebSocket connection by making an API request to /api/chat, which you implemented earlier. As a reminder, it responds with a WebSocket for the client to use that is linked to the WebSocket retained by the server.

```
const wss = document.location.protocol === "http:" ? "ws://" : "wss://";
let connect_url = wss + hostname + `/api/chat?name=${name}`;
```

Rather than HTTP, connecting with WebSockets is handled using the Web-Socket protocol, so the URLs are prefixed with ws or wss, depending on whether the current page is HTTP or HTTPS.

The application also needs to either use the existing chat ID, or generate a new one, which is then appended to both the current page URL in the browser if it's not present, and the API call:

```
if (!chat_id) {
  chat_id = crypto.randomUUID();
  window.history.pushState({}, '', `/?chatId=${chat_id}`);
}

connect_url += `&chatId=${chat_id}`
```

To avoid a page refresh, the application uses window.history.pushState to push a new entry into the history—which will cause the URL to update in the address bar, but avoid a refresh.

With the chat ID set, the browser can connect to the WebSocket:

```javascript
let ws = new WebSocket(connect_url);

$(document).on('click', '#send-msg-btn', function(e) {
  e.preventDefault();

  const msg = $('#chat-msg-input').val();

  ws.send(
    JSON.stringify({ text: msg, name: name })
  )

  $('#chat-msg-input').val('');
})
```

This is as simple as passing the connection URL to the API endpoint that ultimately returns the WebSocket. When the send message button is clicked, it'll use the WebSocket to send a message to the Durable Object. This will then trigger the webSocketMessage method you implemented earlier.

When the user submits their name, the chat interface is hidden, as there's no point showing it in the event the browser fails to connect to the WebSocket. There are several events you can attach to the WebSocket, and this application makes use of two. The first is the open event, that is executed when the connection to the WebSocket is successfully opened:

```javascript
ws.addEventListener('open', event => {
  ws.send(JSON.stringify({ connection_established: true, name: name}));
  $('#connect-container').hide();
  $('#chat-container').show();
})
```

We then send a connection_established message to the WebSocket, which will be broadcast to everyone else in the chat. Additionally, the UI is updated to show the full chat interface, so the user can begin to send and receive messages.

Lastly, the client needs to be informed when a new message is received.

```javascript
ws.addEventListener('message', event => {
  const data = JSON.parse(event.data);

  if (data.type === 'user_message') {
    $('#chat-content').append(`
      <div class="media media-chat">
        <div class="media-body">
          <span class="sender">
            ${data.name}
          </span>
          <p>
            ${data.text}
          </p>
        </div>
      </div>
```

```
      `);
  } else if (data.type === 'metadata') {
    $('#chat-content').append(
      `<div class="media media-meta-day">${data.text}</div>`
    )
  }
});
```

When a message is received by the client WebSocket, it's rendered to the user, with a slight tweak to the format depending on the type of message received.

That's all there is to it, and that rounds out the chapter on Durable Objects.

Durable Object Limits

You can create an unlimited number of Durable Objects, with up to 50GB of storage available per account. The storage limit is adjustable though by contacting Cloudflare.

There's no limit to the amount you can store within a Durable Object, up to your account limit. Each key can be up to 2 KiB, with a key's value able to store up to 128 KiB.

Lastly, each WebSocket message can be up to 1 MiB and each request to a Durable Object can use up to 30 seconds of CPU.

What You've Learned

Real-time communication is definitely not easy, but as you've seen in this chapter, it can be made a lot simpler with Durable Objects.

You learned that Durable Objects are a way to persist objects in your code, and that they are globally unique, so only one can exist with a given ID at any one time. Furthermore, you learned how to handle WebSockets elegantly with Durable Objects, and that they are cost- and energy-efficient due to their ability to hibernate.

You also learned how to render HTML from a Worker, and how that compares to Cloudflare Pages, as well as taking a look at how client-side JavaScript is used to connect to WebSockets.

If you want to see the full code for this project, you can do so on GitHub.[7]

To round out the book, you'll learn how to productionize your applications, covering topics such as custom domains, environments, and first up—automated deployments.

---

7. https://github.com/apeacock1991/serverless-apps-on-cloudflare/tree/main/chat-app-durable-objects

## CHAPTER 14

Automate Workers & Pages Deployments

Throughout the book, you've frequently deployed your applications to Cloudflare using Wrangler. While effective during development, this approach isn't sustainable long term. To ensure safe and consistent deployments, it's essential to adopt CI/CD best practices.

For example, I maintain an application where each deployment includes:

1. Running the test suite.

2. Scraping the latest data needed by the application.

3. Generating checksums of scraped images to force cache invalidation of old images.

4. Uploading the images to R2.

5. Deploying the Worker to Cloudflare.

Although not overly complex, this process must be repeated with every change and on a schedule to keep the data current. Automating deployments offers additional benefits, such as ensuring tests pass before deployment, and providing peace of mind that the application functions correctly.

In a larger company, there are further considerations. For example, an engineer unfamiliar with the application might need to make changes to the codebase. They shouldn't have to know how to deploy the application manually, as this increases the risk of errors or missed steps.

In this chapter, I'll guide you through the various deployment options available on Cloudflare's platform, and you'll automate the deployment of the image analysis application.

Deploy with Git Integration

There are multiple options for automatically deploying changes to your applications on Cloudflare. For Workers, you can either deploy manually from the CLI using Wrangler or automate deployments using tools such as GitHub Actions. You've been using the former throughout the book, and we'll cover the latter later in this chapter.

For Workers and Pages projects, Cloudflare offers its own build platform, compatible with GitHub and GitLab. Connecting a repository to your project is straightforward, but to familiarize yourself with Cloudflare's hosted build system, let's create a new project. Start by creating a new repository on GitHub (or GitLab) with an index.html file in the root, containing the following content:

```
<!DOCTYPE html>
<html>
<body>

<h1>Testing Cloudflare Git Integration</h1>

<p>It works!</p>

</body>
</html>
```

Next, go to the Cloudflare dashboard, click Workers & Pages on the left menu, followed by the Create Application button, and select Pages from the submenu that appears. You will see a screen that looks something like this:

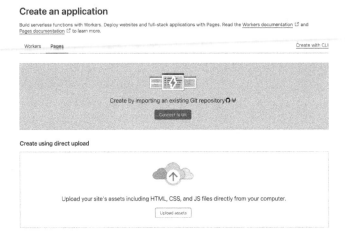

If you prefer to upload your website manually via the dashboard, use the direct upload option on this screen. Note that if you're using a framework like Next.js, you'll need to upload the built files.

To connect your repository, click "Connect to Git" and authorize Cloudflare to access your GitHub or GitLab account. After authorization, you'll see the repositories you granted Cloudflare access to. Select the new repository with the static HTML file, click "Begin setup," and you'll see the following screen:

Project name

```
test-cf-ci-cd
```

Your project will be deployed to **test-cf-ci-cd.pages.dev**.

Production branch

```
main                                    ▼
```

Pushes to this branch automatically trigger deployments to the Production environment. Pushes to all other branches will trigger deployments within the Preview environment.

Build settings (▣ Configuring builds)

If your project uses a static site generator or build tool, set the build instructions for Cloudflare.

Framework preset

```
None                                    ▼
```

Select a framework to prefill recommended settings.

Build command ⓘ

```

```

e.g. npm run build

Build output directory ⓘ

```
/
```

e.g. dist

> Root directory (advanced)

> Environment variables (advanced)

You don't need to make any changes to this screen for a static website like the one you're setting up. However, if you're using a framework or want to adjust your build configuration, here's what each field means:

- *Project name* is pretty self-explanatory; it'll also be used in the URL Cloudflare generates for your project.

- *Production branch* is the branch deployed to production when a commit is pushed. Other branches will be deployed to preview.

- *Framework preset* is the framework you're using. Cloudflare will automatically populate the next two fields. If your framework isn't listed, or you're using a custom one, leave this set to none.

- *Build command* contains the steps to prepare your application for deployment. For example, npx next build for a static Next.js project.

- *Build output directory* is the location of the files produced by the build command. For a static Next.js site, it's out.

- *Root directory* is the directory where Cloudflare executes your build command, useful if your application's files are in a subfolder like src.

- *Environment variables* allows you to set environment-specific variables that are accessible when your application runs. Since no changes are necessary for your simple static HTML website, leave all the settings as default and press "Save and Deploy." After a few seconds, you'll see Cloudflare's build system get to work:

Cloudflare will check out the latest version of the branch you pushed a commit to, run any necessary build commands, and deploy the finalized assets. Click "Continue to Project" at the bottom to see the project overview and access your newly deployed website via the provided URL.

To test the Git integration, create a new commit on the main branch and watch as Cloudflare automatically deploys your site again. If you create a different branch and push a commit, you'll see a preview deployment on the same screen. If there's an open pull request, a comment will be left when deployment completes, informing you of the status and providing a URL to access the deployed code:

Additionally, you can enforce that all pull requests must successfully deploy to preview before they can be merged using status checks.[1]

To configure which branches are deployed and modify the build commands, go to "Settings" under your Pages project, then select "Builds & deployments."

That's all there is to using Cloudflare's Git integration for builds and deployments. If you don't need any custom deployment steps, Cloudflare's Git integration is likely the quickest and easiest way to deploy your Pages projects.

For more complex deployments, where you need to further customize the build process, you can use GitHub Actions. That's what we'll cover next.

Deploy Pages with GitHub Actions

If you cast your mind back to Chapter 11, Produce Messages to a Queue, on page 139, and Chapter 12, Consume Messages from a Queue, on page 151, you built an API that publishes to a queue and a Worker to consume messages from that queue. To maintain the state between these applications, you used a D1 database.

As you further develop the application, you may need to make changes to the D1 database, such as adding columns or creating new tables. When deploying to production, these database migrations must be applied alongside the code deployment.

Historically, Workers and Pages were more separated as products, but this will change as Cloudflare integrates them more closely. Currently, Pages projects can only be deployed using Cloudflare's Git integration, which isn't suitable for this application since it also includes a Worker deployment.

---

1. https://docs.github.com/en/pull-requests/collaborating-with-pull-requests/collaborating-on-repositories-with-code-quality-features/about-status-checks

This is where an external CI/CD tool like GitHub Actions becomes useful. With GitHub Actions, you can create custom workflows triggered by events, such as a merge to the main branch, or the opening of a pull request.

To make use of GitHub Actions, you'll need a free GitHub account. Every GitHub account gets 2,000 minutes of GitHub Actions execution time free per month.

Go to the root directory of the image analysis project and create a new file at .github/workflows/deploy.yml with the following:

```
name: Deploy

on:
  push:
    branches:
      - main
  workflow_dispatch:
```

Once created, the folder structure should look like this:

```
.github/
├── workflows/
│   ├── deploy.yml
frontend/
image-analysis-consumer/
```

GitHub Actions are defined using YAML and have their own specific structure. I'll cover the basics as we go, but the complete workflow syntax is expansive, so if you're keen to learn more, I'd recommend checking out the documentation.[2]

The first thing you define is the name for this particular workflow, this makes it easy to identify in case a repository contains several workflows.

Second, you use the on key to define when this workflow should execute. In this example, the workflow is set to run automatically on any push to the main branch. Additionally, workflow_dispatch allows you to manually run the workflow from the GitHub UI.

There are over thirty events you can use as triggers, most of which allow you to filter for specific events. For instance, in the push event, the workflow is limited to run only for the main branch.[3]

After you've defined when the workflow should be triggered, you can define the logic that needs to be executed by defining jobs as another top-level key:

---

2. https://docs.github.com/en/actions/using-workflows/workflow-syntax-for-github-actions
3. https://docs.github.com/en/actions/using-workflows/events-that-trigger-workflows

```
on:
  push:
    branches:
      - main
  workflow_dispatch:

jobs:
  build_frontend:
    runs-on: ubuntu-latest
    name: Build Frontend
    steps:
      - uses: actions/checkout@v4
      - name: Build
        run: cd frontend && npx @cloudflare/next-on-pages
      - name: Upload Build Artifact
        uses: actions/upload-artifact@v4
        with:
          name: build-artifact
          path: |
            frontend/.vercel/output/static/
```

You can define an unlimited number of jobs per workflow, allowing you to break the workflow into smaller, manageable tasks.

The first job, with an ID of build_frontend, prepares the Next.js application for deployment. It uses the next-on-pages package from Cloudflare to prepare static pages and format Pages Functions for upload.

Each job contains a list of steps that run sequentially to complete the job. Each step can either use another GitHub Action or execute commands against the shell that the GitHub Action runs in.

For this job, there are three steps using a mixture of both:

1. The first step, actions/checkout@v4, uses a GitHub action to check out the latest version of the code for the given repository and branch.

2. Once the code is checked out, change into the frontend directory and execute the build process provided by @cloudflare/next-on-pages. This creates the necessary files for deployment in .vercel/output/static.

3. Finally, you can share files between jobs using another GitHub action, actions/upload-artifact@v4. You provide an artifact name and a list of paths to upload.

Uploading artifacts is essential because each job operates in its own execution environment, completely separate from other jobs. Artifacts provide a way to share state between different jobs.

You might question why we need a separate build job or why we bother splitting the workflow into distinct jobs. These are excellent questions, so let's address them by adding more jobs:

```
jobs:
  build_frontend:
    runs-on: ubuntu-latest
    name: Build Frontend
    steps:
      - uses: actions/checkout@v4
      - name: Build
        run: cd frontend && npx @cloudflare/next-on-pages
      - name: Upload Build Artifact
        uses: actions/upload-artifact@v4
        with:
          name: build-artifact
          path: |
            frontend/.vercel/output/static

  deploy_frontend_preview:
    runs-on: ubuntu-latest
    name: Deploy Frontend (Preview)
    needs: [build_frontend]
    steps:
      - uses: actions/checkout@v4
        with:
          path: repository
      - name: Download Build Artifact
        uses: actions/download-artifact@v4
        with:
          name: build-artifact
      - name: Configure Wrangler
        run: |
          mv repository/frontend/wrangler.preview.toml wrangler.toml && \
          rm -rf repository
      - name: Deploy
        uses: cloudflare/wrangler-action@v3
        with:
          apiToken: ${{ secrets.CLOUDFLARE_API_TOKEN }}
          wranglerVersion: "3.57.1"
          command: pages deploy . --project-name=image-app --branch=preview

  deploy_frontend_production:
    runs-on: ubuntu-latest
    name: Deploy Frontend (Production)
    needs: [build_frontend]
    steps:
      - uses: actions/checkout@v4
        with:
          path: repository
      - name: Download Build Artifact
```

```
  uses: actions/download-artifact@v4
  with:
    name: build-artifact
- name: Configure Wrangler
  run: |
    mv repository/frontend/wrangler.production.toml wrangler.toml && \
    rm -rf repository
- name: Deploy
  uses: cloudflare/wrangler-action@v3
  with:
    apiToken: ${{ secrets.CLOUDFLARE_API_TOKEN }}
    wranglerVersion: "3.57.1"
    command: pages deploy . --project-name=image-app
```

You've added two new jobs with IDs deploy_frontend_preview and deploy_frontend_production. As their IDs suggest, one handles deployment to the preview environment and the other to the production environment.

The structure of these jobs closely resembles that of the build_frontend job. Before you dive into the steps, there's a new key for these jobs called needs.

By default, all jobs in a workflow run in parallel. If you require a specific job to finish before another can start, you use needs to specify dependencies between jobs. This allows you to sequence jobs when necessary.

However, if you're wondering why not just combine all steps into a single job: doing so would eliminate parallel execution, which is often desirable for efficiency in GitHub Actions usage and can lead to faster execution times.

In this workflow example, there are numerous ways to structure it based on your requirements:

1. Have a single job, with all the steps needed to deploy the front end to both preview and production.

2. Have two jobs, one for preview and one for production, that run in parallel.

Both of these would work, but they aren't as optimal as sequencing the jobs. With a single job, all steps run sequentially, but once the build completes, you can deploy in parallel to both preview and production environments. However, this means the entire process is slower due to sequential execution.

On the other hand, using two separate jobs for preview and production deployments ensures that each deployment phase runs concurrently after the build phase. This typically balances the overall execution time of both jobs. However, the downside is increased GitHub Actions usage minutes because you must run the build twice.

If you took arbitrary figures for each step, let's say each build takes five minutes and each deployment takes two minutes, running as two separate jobs, totaling fourteen minutes of GitHub Actions usage. In comparison, sequencing the jobs would only consume nine minutes—five minutes for the build and two minutes each for parallel deployments.

As your application scales and build times increase, optimizing job sequencing becomes more valuable. Starting with optimal job structuring from the beginning effectively minimizes inefficiencies and maximizes your GitHub Actions usage.

For the deployment jobs, the first step is to check out the repository into a subdirectory named repository. Although the application is already built, you still need the Wrangler configuration files for the deployment to know what bindings to use.

Next, you download the build artifact that was uploaded by the build step. This uses the actions/download-artifact action, the sibling to the actions/upload-artifact action.

Before deploying, you need to move the correct Wrangler configuration file into the current working directory. You might notice that there are no wrangler.preview.toml or wrangler.production.toml files, only a single wrangler.toml file. You'll create these shortly, and I'll explain why they're needed.

With all the necessary files in place, you can use the cloudflare/wrangler-action to execute the deployment. This action, maintained by Cloudflare, allows you to run any commands with Wrangler in a GitHub Action. To deploy the front end, execute pages deploy in the current directory (denoted by .) and pass the project name.

The Wrangler action uses Cloudflare's API to deploy your application. To use the API, you need to provide an API token for authentication, which you'll add shortly.

For the preview deployment, an additional flag specifies the branch. Since the Pages deployment environment is determined by the branch name, and the workflow triggers on the main branch, you need to specify another branch for the preview deployment.

You can name this branch anything you like, such as staging, creating a consistent non-production version that mirrors production. When deploying to a branch, Cloudflare prepends the branch name to the URL. If your production URL is image-app.pages.dev, deploying to the staging branch will give you staging.image-app.pages.dev.

To prevent accidental changes to this branch during development, you can set up branch protection rules on GitHub to lock the branch.[4] This ensures that only the GitHub Action can deploy changes to that branch, preventing anyone from pushing commits directly to it.

With the workflow configuration complete to deploy the front end to preview and production, let's add those missing Wrangler configuration files.

Configure Wrangler per Environment

Throughout this book, you've been using a single wrangler.toml file to define all your bindings. This approach works well during development and when deploying from your local machine, but it becomes problematic when automating deployments, especially when using D1.

With the current workflow, you could manage with a single wrangler.toml file that includes environment-specific configurations. During deployment, Cloudflare would detect the correct environment and use the appropriate bindings.

The issue arises when you need to run D1 migrations, which will be covered later in this chapter. This is especially challenging in an enterprise setting with multiple Workers across numerous environments. Although this project is a Pages project with only preview and production environments, relying on a single wrangler.toml file can be messy and error prone. Therefore, I'll show you a scalable approach.

My preferred method is to use multiple TOML files:

- wrangler.toml is used exclusively for local development.

- A wrangler.{environment}.toml file is created for each unique environment, containing the bindings specific to that environment.

For this project, we need both wrangler.preview.toml and wrangler.production.toml files.

Create a new file in the frontend folder called wrangler.preview.toml and add the following:

```
#:schema node_modules/wrangler/config-schema.json
name = "image-app"
compatibility_date = "2024-05-02"
compatibility_flags = ["nodejs_compat"]
pages_build_output_dir = ".vercel/output/static"
```

---

4. https://docs.github.com/en/repositories/configuring-branches-and-merges-in-your-repository/managing-protected-branches/about-protected-branches

```
[[r2_buckets]]
binding = "IMAGE_APP_UPLOADS"
bucket_name = "image-app-uploads-preview"

[[d1_databases]]
binding = "DB" # i.e. available in your Worker on env.DB
database_name = "image-analysis-preview"
database_id = "ec99f664-bfde-4126-95e8-105b8dd196c4"

[[queues.producers]]
queue = "image-analysis-preview"
binding = "ANALYSIS_QUEUE"
```

Ensure all the names and IDs in the wrangler.preview.toml file reflect the resources you created for the preview environment. Once saved, create a second file named wrangler.production.toml with the same format, but replace the names and IDs with those of the production resources.

Next, open wrangler.toml and remove all environment-specific configurations (anything starting with env). Leave the top-level configuration unchanged, pointing to the preview resources. This ensures that during local development, everything is simulated locally, and any issues will affect only the preview environment, not production, should you accidentally run commands remotely.

With the environment-specific Wrangler files created, let's update the workflow to deploy the consumer Workers.

Deploy a Worker with GitHub Actions

Deploying a Worker is even simpler than deploying a Pages project. With a Pages project, you typically need to run the build step first, but with a Worker that build step isn't required.

To deploy your consumer to both preview and production, add the following to the jobs key:

```
deploy_consumer_preview:
  runs-on: ubuntu-latest
  name: Deploy Consumer (Preview)
  steps:
    - uses: actions/checkout@v4
    - name: Deploy
      uses: cloudflare/wrangler-action@v3
      with:
        apiToken: ${{ secrets.CLOUDFLARE_API_TOKEN }}
        wranglerVersion: "3.57.1"
        workingDirectory: image-analysis-consumer
        command: deploy --env preview
```

```
deploy_consumer_production:
  runs-on: ubuntu-latest
  name: Deploy Consumer (Production)
  steps:
    - uses: actions/checkout@v4
    - name: Deploy
      uses: cloudflare/wrangler-action@v3
      with:
        apiToken: ${{ secrets.CLOUDFLARE_API_TOKEN }}
        wranglerVersion: "3.57.1"
        workingDirectory: image-analysis-consumer
        command: deploy --env production
```

All the syntax should look familiar to you, as you've used these two actions already.

To deploy a Worker, you first check out the repository in both jobs. Since checking out a repository is a relatively fast operation, there's no significant benefit in doing it once and using an artifact.

Once the repository is checked out, you use the cloudflare/wrangler-action to run a Worker deploy, passing in the correct environment.

Notice that there are no dependencies for these two jobs, allowing the Workers to deploy concurrently with the front end build and deploy.

The workflow is now complete, but before you run it, you need to provide the workflow with an API token from Cloudflare.

Add Secrets

To prevent your secret information from being leaked in plaintext, GitHub allows you to store secrets on their platform. These secrets are encrypted and won't appear in any output when the action runs.

Before you can add a secret, you need to create a new Cloudflare API token. To do so, follow these steps:

1. Log in to the Cloudflare dashboard (https://dash.cloudflare.com).

2. Click on your user icon in the top right and select My Profile.

3. In the left submenu, click API Tokens, then click the Create Token button.

4. To simplify setting the right permissions, use a predefined template by clicking Use template next to Edit Cloudflare Workers.

Worker Environments vs. Pages Environments

As I alluded to earlier, the Workers and Pages products started out their lives separately. Over time, Cloudflare has merged them closer and closer together. For example, being able to use a wrangler.toml file in a Pages project is a relatively new addition. Based on their regular updates, I fully expect there to be full parity between the two products in future.

One of the remaining differences you'll notice is the disparity between how environments work with Workers and Pages. For Pages project, you only get production and preview. For Workers, you can define an unlimited number of environments, and name them whatever you like.

With Pages having fewer environments available, this can cause problems if you typically use more than two environments—something that's pretty common at an enterprise company. We'll cover ways around this problem in Chapter 15, Deploy to Production, on page 213.

---

5. You can see all the permissions you're granting. Under Account Resources, select your account. If in the future you have multiple accounts, you'll need to select the account you wish to deploy to.

6. Under Zone Resources, select All zones from an account, then select your account again.

Leave the remaining settings as default and click Continue to summary. On the next page, click Create Token. You'll see the token—keep this page open, as you won't be able to retrieve the token once you close it. If you lose the token, you can create another one.

With the API token created, you can store it under your repository so that your actions can access it:

1. Go to your GitHub repository and click on Settings.

2. In the left sidebar, click Secrets and then New repository secret.

3. Name the secret CLOUDFLARE_API_TOKEN and paste the token into the value field.

4. Click Add secret.

This secret will be available to any GitHub action in this repository. If you have numerous repositories you want to want to deploy to Cloudflare that sit under an organization in GitHub, you can add a secret to an organization to save you adding it to each individual repository.[5]

With the secret added, let's run the action.

Run a GitHub Action

To test everything, you have two options: push a new commit to the main branch or use the GitHub UI. I'll cover using the UI since it's less familiar. Before proceeding, commit and push your changes to trigger the action.

First, create the Pages project manually as the action cannot do this. If you haven't deployed this project yet, run npm run deploy in the frontend folder, setting the production branch to main when prompted. This step isn't needed for the Worker.

To manually run a workflow, go to your GitHub repository and click Actions at the top. You'll see all the defined workflows on the left and recent runs on the right—if you committed your changes, you might see one running now.

From the left menu, click the Deploy action you created. On the right, click the Run workflow button, leave the branch as main, and hit the green Run workflow button.

This is how you manually trigger any Action that allows workflow_dispatch in its triggers. After a few seconds, the action will start to execute and appear in the list of workflow runs on this page. If you click on it, you can watch as the Action is executed. GitHub shows a nice visualization of the jobs and their dependencies in its UI for each job that runs.

This triggers any Action that allows workflow_dispatch in its triggers. After a few seconds, the action starts and appears in the workflow runs list. Click on it to watch its execution, with GitHub showing a visualization of jobs and their dependencies in the UI. (This is shown in the image on the next page.)

Jobs that run in parallel are in the same box, and dependencies between jobs are shown by lines connecting the boxes. The flow is left to right, so any box connected to its left depends on those jobs.

As jobs run, they are marked active, then successful or failed once finished. If a job fails, you can click on it to view the logs.

---

5.   https://docs.github.com/en/codespaces/managing-codespaces-for-your-organization/managing-development-environment-secrets-for-your-repository-or-organization#adding-secrets-for-an-organization

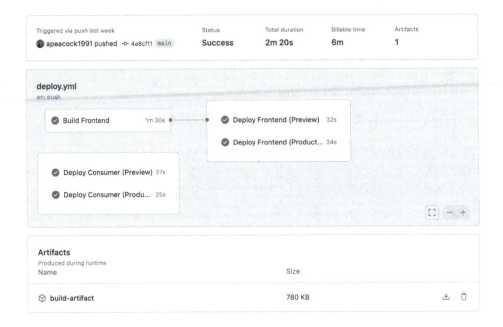

The UI also shows the commit being actioned, the total duration, and the billing time used. You can see and download any artifacts created during the workflow, useful for debugging to check the artifact's contents.

After a few minutes, the workflow will complete, and both your Pages project and Workers will be deployed.

If you have a sharp memory, you might be thinking you're still missing a step: applying database migrations, and you'd be right!

Apply Database Migrations

To complete the workflow, you need to execute database migrations before deploying the latest versions of the front end and consumer. The order is crucial, as the new code might depend on new columns or tables, making it essential to run migrations first.

For this flow to work, it's important to ensure your database changes are backward-compatible, otherwise you may get a brief outage between the migration running and the latest code being deployed. That's just good engineering practice though, and regardless of the platform, you're always going to have a race condition that needs to be considered between database changes and code changes.

As with other parts of the deployment process, you can use two new jobs to apply any database migrations. Add the following to the jobs key:

```
apply_database_migrations_preview:
  runs-on: ubuntu-latest
  name: Apply Database Migrations (Preview)
  needs: [build_frontend]
  steps:
    - uses: actions/checkout@v4
    - name: Configure Wrangler
      run: mv -f frontend/wrangler.preview.toml frontend/wrangler.toml
    - name: Run Database Migrations
      uses: cloudflare/wrangler-action@v3
      with:
        apiToken: ${{ secrets.CLOUDFLARE_API_TOKEN }}
        wranglerVersion: "3.57.1"
        workingDirectory: "frontend"
        command: d1 migrations apply image-analysis-preview --remote
apply_database_migrations_production:
  runs-on: ubuntu-latest
  name: Apply Database Migrations (Production)
  needs: [build_frontend]
  steps:
    - uses: actions/checkout@v4
    - name: Configure Wrangler
      run: mv -f frontend/wrangler.production.toml frontend/wrangler.toml
    - name: Run Database Migrations
      uses: cloudflare/wrangler-action@v3
      with:
        apiToken: ${{ secrets.CLOUDFLARE_API_TOKEN }}
        wranglerVersion: "3.57.1"
        workingDirectory: "frontend"
        command: d1 migrations apply image-analysis --remote
```

The syntax for adding database migrations is similar to other jobs. Note the needs key, which sequences the deployment steps. If the build fails, the database migrations should not be applied, as you can't deploy the application, which would result in an out-of-sync state.

Assuming the build job passes, three steps are needed to execute a database migration:

1. Checkout the code from the repository, as the artifact from the build step lacks the migrations folder and Wrangler configuration files.
2. Replace the current wrangler.toml with an environment-specific file: wrangler.preview.toml for preview or wrangler.production.toml for production.
3. Use the cloudflare/wrangler-action to run the D1 migration, specifying the appropriate database name based on the environment.

Additionally, you need to update the deployment steps to depend on the database migration steps. Under the deploy_frontend_preview and deploy_frontend_production jobs, update the needs key to needs: [apply_database_migrations_preview] and needs: [apply_database_migrations_production] respectively.

You also need to update the deploy_consumer_preview and deploy_consumer_production jobs to depend on the database migration steps too. This will ensure that any database migrations are applied prior to any application code being updated.

Once again, you can commit your changes and push to GitHub. If you were to take a look at how the workflow displays now, it would look something like this:

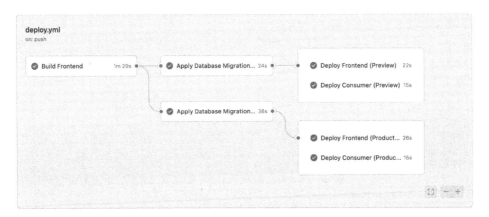

As you can see, the workflow has evolved significantly. There are now three distinct parts: build, migrate, and deploy. Plus, rather than the consumers being deployed right away, they now wait for the database migrations to pass.

To verify everything is working as expected and that database migrations are applied, create a new D1 migration, commit and push it, and then check the Cloudflare dashboard to confirm the migration has been applied after the action has run.

What You've Learned

In this chapter, you learned all about automated deployments of your Cloudflare projects. You created a new project and saw how to make use of the build tools Cloudflare provides via its platform, followed by creating a GitHub Action to deploy from GitHub.

We covered the core structure of a GitHub Action, with on used to define the scenarios where the action should run, and jobs used to create a grouping of steps to complete part of a workflow. Furthermore, you learned how to create dependencies between different jobs, as well as how to optimize your jobs and how you can run jobs in parallel.

Deployment is just one part of preparing your applications for production. In the next chapter, we'll cover a number of other things to think about when deploying your application to end users.

## CHAPTER 15

Deploy to Production

As we near the end of the book, you may already be dreaming about the next project that you can deploy to Cloudflare. Hopefully, your experience with Cloudflare has been enjoyable, motivating you to leverage its capabilities in future endeavors.

While the projects so far have been in development, utilizing auto-generated URLs without concerns about DNS, analytics, or email addresses, the next step is deploying a completed project to a custom domain, optimized for efficiently serving traffic.

In this chapter, we'll explore deploying a project to production, ensuring optimal performance for end users accessing your website, whether it's an API or a full-fledged site. Cloudflare's strength lies in speed and security, offering a comprehensive array of features. While we won't look deeply into every aspect, this chapter serves as a guide to showcase the diverse functionality available, with some more specialized features.

Let's get started with the part of a project a lot of engineers love: buying and configuring a custom domain.

Register and Transfer Domains

No project is complete until it's hosted on its own domain. For me at least, there's no better stage when working on a project than when I can access all my hard work on a professional-looking custom domain.

You may have already purchased a domain, or wish to purchase a new one, and we'll cover each of those scenarios.

If you don't have a domain yet, start by logging into the Cloudflare dashboard. In the left menu, find the Domain Registration option. This section allows you to manage existing domains, transfer a domain to Cloudflare, or register a new domain. Opt for the last option, and you'll encounter a straightforward screen for searching and registering a new domain.

If you purchased one, the domain would appear in the Manage Domains section, automatically configured to work with Cloudflare. This quick setup enables immediate use with your project. Choosing Cloudflare for domain registration also comes with a price promise—guaranteeing wholesale pricing, making it unlikely you'll find cheaper options elsewhere.[1] Additionally, it eliminates the need for manual DNS configuration to point to Cloudflare.

If you've already registered the domain elsewhere, it's easy to transfer it to Cloudflare using the Transfer Domains link in the menu. The process is a little annoying, and involves jumping through a few hoops. In short, you tell Cloudflare what domains you wish to transfer, your current registrar will need to confirm the transfer, often via auto-generated emails, and then Cloudflare will transfer the domain across.

If you want to leave your domain where it is, that's perfectly fine, and for now you don't need to do anything in the Domain Registration section. All the changes required to point a domain to Cloudflare will be covered in the next section.

Add a Custom Domain to a Project

At this point, you must have a domain registered to set up a custom domain. Whether you just registered one with Cloudflare, or plan to point the domain to Cloudflare using DNS, the key part is you need a domain.

I'm going to use the AI image application we built in the last few chapters as an example, but the steps are largely the same for a Worker and a Pages project.

To get started, navigate to the project under Workers & Pages. Near the top of the screen, you'll see a tab called Custom Domains, which you'll need to click, followed by Set up a custom domain. A little form will appear; you just need to type the custom domain that you want to use for this project.

If the domain is registered with Cloudflare, the next screen will confirm you want to add a DNS record to that domain, which you do, and then everything will work after a few minutes.

If the domain is registered externally, you need to add what's called a DNS zone for the new domain. A DNS zone is a section of the DNS namespace that is managed by a specific organization or administrator. A zone may contain

---

1.   https://blog.cloudflare.com/cloudflare-registrar

a single domain (e.g. example.com) or it may contain many domains (e.g., foo.example.com, example.com, and bar.example.com).

When entering a domain into the custom domain form, Cloudflare will detect that the domain isn't registered with Cloudflare, and that no zone yet exists for it. It'll present you with a button to add a new zone. Make sure you pick the Free plan when asked. Once the zone is added, you'll need to follow the steps Cloudflare asks you to. Most commonly, they'll ask you to update the Nameservers for your domain to point to Cloudflare.

This may take up to twenty-four hours to update, depending on what registrar you use. You can check the status, or ask Cloudflare to check the status, under the Websites menu item on the left. The Websites page allows you to see all the domains associated with your Cloudflare account, including ones that are simply pointing at Cloudflare, alongside any that were registered by Cloudflare.

Once the new domain has a little tick by it on the Websites page, you can return to the project's custom domain settings, and add the custom domain.

Whichever route you choose, you should now be able to see your project hosted on the custom domain of your choice. Cloudflare will take care of the SSL too, so you don't need to register any SSL certificates, and your project, at least by default, will be hosted over a secure connection.

To set up a custom domain for a Worker, the steps are almost identical. The only difference is where you find the custom domain configuration, which is under Triggers within each Worker.

With your project now live and available to the public, there are some considerations for local development, and making changes to your application without impacting production. This is where environments come in.

Manage Different Environments

At a few stages in the book, particularly when it comes to Pages projects, we've touched on environments. One of the areas I believe Cloudflare has some work to do, or perhaps I've not found a good way of working with yet, is environments.

When I say environments, I am talking about the different places where you deploy your applications. Commonly in enterprise companies, there are standardized ways to deploy applications, depending on where you're at in the software development life cycle.

For example, when working on new code locally, you might call that the "development" environment. If you want to test your code further, in a remote environment, before you merge your code to the main branch, you might deploy to an environment called "integration." When you merge the code to the main branch, you might first deploy to a staging environment, or a pre-prod environment, and finally to the production environment.

Each environment should be completely separate, with no data or interactions between environments. It should be impossible for staging data to go anywhere near production, and vice versa.

With Cloudflare Pages, there are just two environments: preview and production. In this case, production is naturally for production, but preview has to cover all the other non-production environments, such as integration and staging. This causes some friction, because you are effectively limited to one non-production environment, as you can only realistically bind once per use case (e.g., if you need a D1 database, and bind it to DATABASE, that's it—you can't have separate ones for integration and staging).

Moving over to Workers, it's a completely different story. Workers make heavy use of the wrangler.toml file, which actually supports creating different environments. Let's take the Photo API you built in Chapter 4, Persist Data with D1, on page 33; its wrangler.toml file ended up looking something like this:

```
name = "photo-service"
main = "src/index.ts"
compatibility_date = "2023-04-07"

[[ d1_databases ]]
binding = "DB"
database_name = "photo-service"
database_id = "276bd070-ced5-4552-8d4a-07a151764713"
```

Currently, no environments are configured, so there's just one single environment, de facto making it production. If you wanted to create different environments, let's say development, staging, and production, you would do as follows:

```
name = "photo-service"
main = "src/index.ts"
compatibility_date = "2023-04-07"

d1_databases = [
  {
    binding = "DB",
    database_name = "photo-service-development",
    database_id = "xxx"
  }
]
```

```
[env.staging]
d1_databases = [
  {
    binding = "DB",
    database_name = "photo-service-staging",
    database_id = "yyy"
  }
]

[env.production]
d1_databases = [
  {
    binding = "DB",
    database_name = "photo-service-production",
    database_id = "zzz"
  }
]
```

With environments, there's a default top-level environment, that the above file is using to represent development. I choose to use the top-level environment for development purely because it's the default, and development is the safest default to assume.

Underneath the top-level environment, you'll notice two environments defined: staging and production. There's no defined list of allowed names; you can use whatever you prefer. To create a new environment, you add a line in your wrangler.toml with the format [env.<NAME>] where <NAME> needs to be replaced with the name for your environment.

Anything defined after that will belong to that environment, until another environment line is defined.

Wrangler uses the notion of inheritable and non-inheritable keys. The majority of the keys can be inherited from the top level, which you can see happening above, as there was no need to redefine name, main, or compatibility_date. However, keys such as bindings need to be defined per environment, as they cannot be inherited. This is quite handy, as it means if you forget to include a key, it's not going to accidentally access another environment's data.

You can find a full list of possible keys, and whether they are inheritable or not, in Cloudflare's Wrangler documentation.[2]

If you have a custom domain configured for this Worker, you need to additionally define a route for each environment. (This is shown on the next page.)

---

2. https://developers.cloudflare.com/workers/wrangler/configuration/#inheritable-keys

```
name = "photo-service"
main = "src/index.ts"
compatibility_date = "2023-04-07"

d1_databases = [
  {
    binding = "DB",
    database_name = "photo-service-development",
    database_id = "xxx"
  }
]

route = 'dev.example.com/*'

[env.staging]
d1_databases = [
  {
    binding = "DB",
    database_name = "photo-service-staging",
    database_id = "yyy"
  }
]

route = 'staging.example.com/*'

[env.production]
d1_databases = [
  {
    binding = "DB",
    database_name = "photo-service-production",
    database_id = "zzz"
  }
]

route = 'example.com/*'
```

With the configuration complete, you can now deploy to any of these environments when using wrangler deploy -e staging. If you provide no environment flag, the top-level environment will be used.

I would recommend arranging your environments differently depending on whether you're working on your own side projects, or whether it's a more complex enterprise environment.

For solo work on side projects, I don't worry about environments at all. I configure everything at the top level of wrangler.toml, and for any development work, I do that almost exclusively locally, making use of Wrangler's excellent local emulation capabilities. When I'm finished and ready to deploy, I run a deploy locally, as you've been doing throughout the book.

That works perfectly for side projects, but that sort of setup isn't going to work in more complex enterprise settings. If you followed that same practice, engineers would accidentally deploy to production left, right, and center.

My recommendation is to not make use of environments in wrangler.toml, purely because they don't consistently span across Pages and Workers. Instead, for development work, try to do all of that locally where possible. The vast majority of Cloudflare's functionality is available locally, with the notable exception being Workers AI.

When deploying to staging and production, create explicit accounts in Cloudflare for each that are completely separate. When you want to deploy to staging, you deploy to the staging account, and when you want to deploy to production, you deploy to the production account. This ensures everything is kept separate, as well as preventing engineers from being able to deploy to staging and production directly.

If local development for engineers becomes problematic, or you simply want to enable them to run their applications on Cloudflare, each engineer will automatically be created their own account for enterprise accounts. Each engineer can then deploy to their own account and not worry about impacting staging or production. The only caveat is each account, in terms of billing, is completely separate. Therefore, if you're using paid features, you'll need to pay $5/month for each engineer.

You now know some of the ways to use environments, both for local development and for setting up other environments too, such as staging and production. Once you've deployed to production, you'll want to be able to easily observe your application through metrics and logs, which is what we'll cover next.

View and Query Logs

Deploying your application to production requires a robust system for monitoring user activity and identifying potential errors. While observability is a vast topic, we'll focus on one fundamental aspect: logs.

In the Cloudflare dashboard, when you access a Worker or Pages project, you'll find high-level metrics presented on graphs. These metrics include the number of requests, error occurrences, and request processing times.

As discussed in Chapter 8, Cache Data with KV, on page 97, you can live-tail logs to observe real-time log generation, aiding in development and debugging in production. However, to effectively debug in production, it's crucial to be notified when an error occurs.

In September 2024, Cloudflare released Workers Logs off the back of their acquisition of Baselime earlier in the year. At the time of writing, it's in beta, but allows you to store logs for your Workers for up to seven days on the Workers Paid plan, or three days on the free plan. Additionally, you can use a simple-yet-powerful interface on the Cloudflare dashboard to query through your logs.

All you need to do to enable logs for a Worker is to add the following to your wrangler.toml:

```
[observability]
enabled = true
head_sampling_rate = 1 # optional. default = 1.
```

After the Worker is deployed, you can go to that Worker's page on the Cloudflare dashboard, click the Logs tab, and off you go. When Workers Logs exits beta, there will be a cost for storing logs beyond the free allowance. On the free plan, you get 200,000 logs per day for free, with any logs beyond that point not being stored. On the $5 Workers Paid plan, you get 20 million logs per month included, with every 1 million logs after that costing $0.60.

If your Worker is particularly busy, the costs could quickly add up. That's where the head_sampling_rate can be helpful, which allows you to determine the percent of your logs that are stored. You can set a value from 0 to 1, with 1 storing 100 percent of logs, and 0 storing 0 percent of logs. If you wanted to store 50 percent of logs, you'd set the value to 0.5.

If you already have a platform you use to store and query your logs, you can use Workers Logpush to send the logs to a third-party provider.[3] Cloudflare allows you to push to a number of supported platforms, including New Relic, Datadog, and Splunk.

Additional providers are available, as realistically they just need to be able to accept a stream of data.[4]

With your logs now flowing freely, let's look at an option available to you once you have a custom domain: Workers Routes.

---

3. https://developers.cloudflare.com/workers/observability/logs/logpush/
4. https://developers.cloudflare.com/logs/get-started/enable-destinations/

Define Advanced Routes for Workers

In Chapter 1, Deploy Your First Cloudflare Worker, on page 1, we discussed the different approaches to build serverless applications. Throughout the book, you've been building what I would call "monolithic" functions, where a single Worker handles every request to a given domain. One of the alternative approaches is to have different Workers for different paths on the same domain.

For example, if a request hits example.com/foo it invokes the FooWorker, and if it hits example.com/bar it hits the BarWorker. When developing locally, or even developing on an auto-generated domain in development, this simply isn't possible, as it requires a DNS zone to exist on your Cloudflare account.

Under Websites in the Cloudflare dashboard, click on any website you've set up. On the left menu on the next page, click Workers Routes.

On this page, you can configure any number of specific routes for the website you picked. Going back to the example at the start of this section, if you wanted to set up that routing, you would click Add Route, and be shown the following screen:

To configure example.com/foo to hit a Worker named FooWorker, you would type example.com/foo in the Route box, and then select FooWorker from the dropdown. You'd repeat the process for the other endpoint, effectively allowing you to route to different Workers based on the URL requested. The Route box supports the use of wildcards too, so you could route *.example.com to a Worker, to route any subdomains to a given Worker.

I personally find this makes your architecture more complex and difficult to understand, and often creates more problems than it solves, but it's worthwhile knowing it's an option if you ever need it.

However, there are use cases where I find it incredibly powerful. Let's say you host your landing pages on a third-party tool that doesn't support A/B testing. To enable you to A/B test your landing pages, you can put Cloudflare in front of your website and it'll just act as a reverse proxy, with benefits like bot detection, DDoS protection, and caching. Using Workers Routes, you can intercept specific paths, such as your landing pages, and display different content to different users, and then monitor which one performs better.

There are a few more sections to go for this chapter, and while we're not going in depth, I think it's valuable for you to know these little tools and tricks Cloudflare has up its sleeve, as they've come in really handy for me in the past. Next up, we have one of Cloudflare's newer features: gradual deployments.

Deploy Changes Gradually

Let's say you are deploying a big or risky change on a high-traffic website. You're pretty confident everything is going to work as it should, but wouldn't it be handy to be able to send a small percentage of traffic to the new code to check, before rolling out for everyone?

That's where gradual deployments come in for Workers. Rather than simply running a deploy, as you have been in this book, you can create a new deployment for the new version of your Worker and set the percentage of traffic you want to send to the new version of your Worker.

For example, you might choose to send 10 percent of traffic to the new version of your code, and 90 percent to the old version. You can then inspect the logs, which can be tied to specific versions of your Worker, to make sure everything is looking as you expect, and there are no errors being raised.

All being well, you can update the new version of your Worker to serve a higher percentage of traffic—let's say 50 percent—and then again make sure everything looks as expected. Finally, you can update the split so that 100 percent of traffic goes to the latest version.

While this feature isn't needed for every deployment, it's incredibly useful to have available so you can gradually roll out changes if you need to. At present, it's only available for Workers, with support for gradual Pages deployments coming in the future.

The next feature is one of my personal favorites, and it allows you to secure all, or part, of your website seamlessly behind single sign-on providers. Let's take a look.

Configure Access to Your Applications

At the start of its journey, Cloudflare was primarily a security company. Its focus was on being a proxy between its client websites and the world, ensuring their websites were protected from bad actors.

As you might expect, they still excel in this area. For example, any website or Worker hosted on Cloudflare is automatically given DDoS protection.

One of the more useful aspects of their security offering is the ability to customize who has access to your applications, using Access Policies.[5] You can configure a number of identity providers (IdP), such as Google, Facebook, or LinkedIn, and then use the information retrieved from that identity provider to approve or deny requests to your application.[6]

For example, let's say your application exposes some back office functionality, allowing you to manage your website's users. Perhaps you run a website that allows a user to sign up to a subscription, and they want to cancel or refund their purchase. You need an area of the website that provides a UI that only you and other employees can access.

You could spend time setting up your own authentication, storing emails and passwords, or using an external provider like Auth0, but instead, you could leverage Cloudflare's capabilities to do so.

All that would be required is to configure the integration with an identity provider, such as Google, and then define an Access Policy that only allows certain email addresses (or email address domains, if you're using a consistent domain for employee emails).

The setup is surprisingly easy, and I've included links to the key documentation in the footnotes.

---

5.   https://developers.cloudflare.com/cloudflare-one/policies/access/

6.   https://developers.cloudflare.com/cloudflare-one/identity/idp-integration/

Handle Emails

Cloudflare doesn't natively support mailboxes or setting up email addresses. If you want to send emails from your custom domain, you'll need an external provider for that. However, if you simply want to receive email, Cloudflare supports email forwarding. You go to the website you want to forward emails from in the Cloudflare dashboard, and click Emails on the left menu.

After clicking "Get started," you'll be presented with a screen like this one:

Get started with Email Routing

This process will guide you through creating a custom address and configuring your DNS to enable Email Routing for this domain.

Create a custom address

Add the custom address you want to receive emails in and the action to take. New destination addresses will be sent a confirmation before incoming emails are routed.

Custom address

[   ] @ example.com

Action ⓘ
Send to an email

Destination

[× ▾]

Required.

──────────────────────────────────────

[Exit] [Create and continue]   [Skip getting started]

Simply enter the email address you wish to receive email to on your custom domain in the first box, and enter the email address to forward mail to in the second box, and Cloudflare will handle the rest.

Additionally, if you want to accept emails and handle them programmatically, you can set up email addresses (or use the catch-all option) that trigger a Worker when an email is received.[7]

Analytics, Security, and Speed

The last section is a bit of a "catch all" for everything else that's left, but it's really small and they're mostly nice-to-haves, but again, it's important to know this functionality exists.

───────────────

7.   https://developers.cloudflare.com/email-routing/email-workers/

Under any website hosted on Cloudflare, you have a plethora of options available to you. The last ones worth covering have the following headings:

- Analytics allows you to see basic metrics about your website, such as the number of visitors, the number of requests your website handled, and the amount of bandwidth used. You can also see which country traffic is coming from, as well as see if Cloudflare blocked any attacks against your website.

- Security allows you to view and tweak key security aspects provided by Cloudflare, such as the Web Application Firewall (WAF), bot protection, and DDoS protection.

- Speed allows you to control any performance optimizations that Cloudflare can automatically apply to your website. There are many options in here, covering everything from what HTTP and TLS version to use; to automatically minifying HTML, CSS, and JS; to optimizing fonts, early hints, and so much more. Just out in beta, there's an observatory tool under the Speed section that will run tests against your website, and detect any optimizations that could be enabled. Additionally in beta, there's Speed Brain. This makes use of the Speculation Rules API in the browser to preload pages before a user clicks on a link, making the page load incredibly fast (likely from browser cache). This is enabled by default for all new domains.

- Rules allow you to define behavior in certain scenarios. For example, you might want to redirect users who access your website without the www subdomain to the www subdomain—this is easily achieved with a redirect rule. In cases where you're using Cloudflare as a reverse proxy, you can make use of Cloudflare's global cache to serve web pages directly from cache rather than hitting the origin server, such as your WordPress blog. Added in October 2024, compression rules allow you to tweak the compression algorithm applied, with zstd being added most recently—an improvement upon Brotli.

What You've Learned

In this chapter, we took a whistle-stop tour through preparing your application for production. The primary focus was ensuring you know how to register, or point, a custom domain to Cloudflare, so you can host your applications on their own custom domains.

You also learned how to set up different environments for your projects, and an approach to deal with larger projects, using different Cloudflare accounts for staging and production. Moving to production would be terrifying without being able to see what's going on inside your application, so you also learned how to push logs to external observability vendors from your projects.

Additionally, we covered a series of nifty features Cloudflare gives you access to once your custom domain is routed through their network, such as email routing, Worker Routes, and speed optimizations.

Container-Based Applications Coming in 2025

At Cloudflare's Birthday Week in September 2024, they announced they're working on allowing engineers to deploy containers to Cloudflare's global network for the first time. As covered throughout the book, it's currently only possible to deploy applications to Cloudflare using their Worker platform that supports the V8 runtime.

That will change in 2025. You'll be able to deploy containers to Cloudflare alongside Workers, using technologies such as Docker. What this looks like in detail is not known, but I suspect it'll power mostly asynchronous use cases where you need heavier processing and can live with a cold start. They are already being used internally for a number of Cloudflare products.

At the time of writing, the only information available is a blog post, https://blog.cloudflare.com/container-platform-preview. I highly recommend reading it if you're interested in deploying containers.

This is the final chapter in the book, so if you made it to this point, thank you so much for reading. I hope you enjoyed reading it as much as I enjoyed writing it. You're now armed with all the knowledge you need to build serverless applications on Cloudflare. You've learned everything from creating Workers and full stack applications with Pages, to how to persist data in D1 and store files in R2, and everything in between.

If you have any questions, or simply want to chat about serverless or Cloudflare, don't hesitate to reach out to me via one of the following methods:

- Email: ashley@technicalbookclub.com
- Twitter: @_ashleypeacock

Index

Thank you!

We hope you enjoyed this book and that you're already thinking about what you want to learn next. To help make that decision easier, we're offering you this gift.

Head on over to https://pragprog.com right now, and use the coupon code BUYANOTHER2024 to save 30% on your next ebook. Offer is void where prohibited or restricted. This offer does not apply to any edition of *The Pragmatic Programmer* ebook.

And if you'd like to share your own expertise with the world, why not propose a writing idea to us? After all, many of our best authors started off as our readers, just like you. With up to a 50% royalty, world-class editorial services, and a name you trust, there's nothing to lose. Visit https://pragprog.com/become-an-author/ today to learn more and to get started.

Thank you for your continued support. We hope to hear from you again soon!

The Pragmatic Bookshelf

SAVE 30%!
Use coupon code
BUYANOTHER2024

Creating Software with Modern Diagramming Techniques

Diagrams communicate relationships more directly and clearly than words ever can. Using only text-based markup, create meaningful and attractive diagrams to document your domain, visualize user flows, reveal system architecture at any desired level, or refactor your code. With the tools and techniques this book will give you, you'll create a wide variety of diagrams in minutes, share them with others, and revise and update them immediately on the basis of feedback. Adding diagrams to your professional vocabulary will enable you to work through your ideas quickly when working on your own code or discussing a proposal with colleagues.

Ashley Peacock
(156 pages) ISBN: 9781680509830. $29.95
https://pragprog.com/book/apdiag

Serverless Single Page Apps

Don't waste your time building an application server. See how to build low-cost, low-maintenance, highly available, serverless single page web applications that scale into the millions of users at the click of a button. Quickly build reliable, well-tested single page apps that stay up and running 24/7 using Amazon Web Services. Avoid messing around with middle-tier infrastructure and get right to the web app your customers want.

Ben Rady
(212 pages) ISBN: 9781680501490. $24
https://pragprog.com/book/brapps

Test-Driven React, Second Edition

Turn your React project requirements into tests and get the feedback you need faster than ever before. Combine the power of testing, linting, and typechecking directly in your coding environment to iterate on React components quickly and fearlessly!

Trevor Burnham
(172 pages) ISBN: 9798888650653. $45.95
https://pragprog.com/book/tbreact2

Your Code as a Crime Scene, Second Edition

Jack the Ripper and legacy codebases have more in common than you'd think. Inspired by forensic psychology methods, you can apply strategies to identify problems in your existing code, assess refactoring direction, and understand how your team influences the software architecture. With its unique blend of criminal psychology and code analysis, *Your Code as a Crime Scene* arms you with the techniques you need to take on any codebase, no matter what programming language you use.

Adam Tornhill
(336 pages) ISBN: 9798888650325. $53.95
https://pragprog.com/book/atcrime2

A Common-Sense Guide to Data Structures and Algorithms in Python, Volume 1

If you thought data structures and algorithms were all just theory, you're missing out on what they can do for your Python code. Learn to use Big O notation to make your code run faster by orders of magnitude. Choose from data structures such as hash tables, trees, and graphs to increase your code's efficiency exponentially. With simple language and clear diagrams, this book makes this complex topic accessible, no matter your background. Every chapter features practice exercises to give you the hands-on information you need to master data structures and algorithms for your day-to-day work.

Jay Wengrow
(502 pages) ISBN: 9798888650356. $57.95
https://pragprog.com/book/jwpython

A Common-Sense Guide to Data Structures and Algorithms in JavaScript, Volume 1

If you thought data structures and algorithms were all just theory, you're missing out on what they can do for your JavaScript code. Learn to use Big O notation to make your code run faster by orders of magnitude. Choose from data structures such as hash tables, trees, and graphs to increase your code's efficiency exponentially. With simple language and clear diagrams, this book makes this complex topic accessible, no matter your background. Every chapter features practice exercises to give you the hands-on information you need to master data structures and algorithms for your day-to-day work.

Jay Wengrow
(514 pages) ISBN: 9798888650646. $69.95
https://pragprog.com/book/jwjavascript

The Pragmatic Bookshelf

The Pragmatic Bookshelf features books written by professional developers for professional developers. The titles continue the well-known Pragmatic Programmer style and continue to garner awards and rave reviews. As development gets more and more difficult, the Pragmatic Programmers will be there with more titles and products to help you stay on top of your game.

Visit Us Online

This Book's Home Page
https://pragprog.com/book/apapps
Source code from this book, errata, and other resources. Come give us feedback, too!

Keep Up-to-Date
https://pragprog.com
Join our announcement mailing list (low volume) or follow us on Twitter @pragprog for new titles, sales, coupons, hot tips, and more.

New and Noteworthy
https://pragprog.com/news
Check out the latest Pragmatic developments, new titles, and other offerings.

Save on the ebook

Save on the ebook versions of this title. Owning the paper version of this book entitles you to purchase the electronic versions at a terrific discount.

PDFs are great for carrying around on your laptop—they are hyperlinked, have color, and are fully searchable. Most titles are also available for the iPhone and iPod touch, Amazon Kindle, and other popular e-book readers.

Send a copy of your receipt to support@pragprog.com and we'll provide you with a discount coupon.

Contact Us

Online Orders:	*https://pragprog.com/catalog*
Customer Service:	*support@pragprog.com*
International Rights:	*translations@pragprog.com*
Academic Use:	*academic@pragprog.com*
Write for Us:	*http://write-for-us.pragprog.com*

www.ingramcontent.com/pod-product-compliance
Lightning Source LLC
LaVergne TN
LVHW081339050326
832903LV00024B/1207